101 sparkling necklaces

101
sparkling
necklaces

Cheryl Owen

NEW
HOLLAND

First published in 2007
This paperback edition first published in 2008 by
New Holland Publishers (UK) Ltd
London • Cape Town • Sydney • Auckland

Garfield House
86–88 Edgware Road
London W2 2EA
United Kingdom
www.newhollandpublishers.com

80 McKenzie Street
Cape Town 8001
South Africa

Unit 1, 66 Gibbes Street
Chatswood
NSW 2067
Australia

218 Lake Road
Northcote
Auckland
New Zealand

ISBN 978 1 84773 289 7

Senior Editor: Corinne Masciocchi
Designer: Sue Rose
Photographer: Shona Wood
Production: Hazel Kirkman
Editorial Direction: Rosemary Wilkinson

2 4 6 8 10 9 7 5 3 1

Reproduction by Colour Scan Overseas, Singapore
Printed and bound by Craft Print International Pte Ltd, Singapore

Contents

Introduction

Introduction

 Making your own necklaces is great fun and wonderful creations are surprisingly easy and inexpensive to achieve. Only basic equipment is necessary and the choice of fabulous beads and other materials, such as shells and feathers is endless.

This book has ideas for all tastes and styles, and each project is accompanied by easy-to-follow, step-by-step instructions. The same basic techniques occur throughout the book and will help you create jewellery to a very professional standard.

All the projects make lovely gifts and it is easy to adapt the instructions to make additional matching items: simply make shorter versions for bracelets or hang co-ordinating beads on earring wires. Let your imagination run free and be inspired by the masses of innovative ideas within these pages to create your very personal stunning designs.

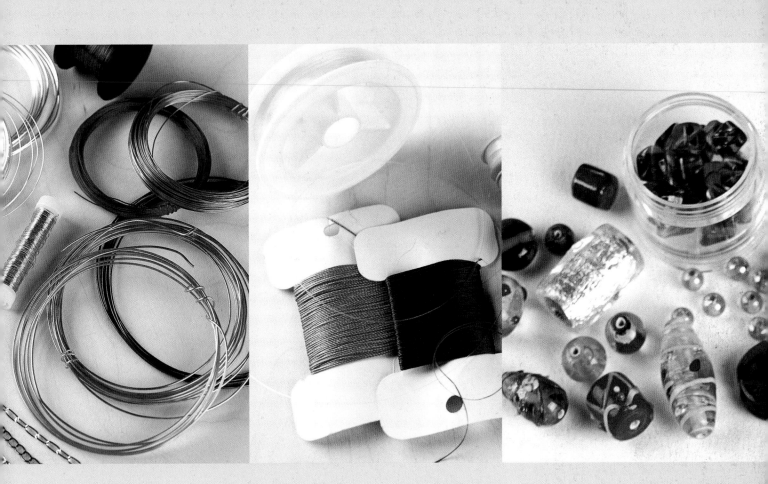

Materials and equipment

Beads and pendants

It is the wonderful variety of beads that are widely available that makes necklace-making so much fun – and addictive! There are many specialist bead shops and the internet makes beads from all over the world easily accessible. Beading need not be an expensive venture – a few exotic and costly beads can be shown to great effect amongst smaller, inexpensive beads on a necklace. Recycle beads from broken or out-dated jewellery or buy pieces at car boot sales to take apart and give a new lease of life to.

Glass beads

Mass produced beads are pressed or moulded in all sorts of shapes and sizes and come in a myriad range of transparent and opaque colours. The fabulous hand-crafted glass beads that are created today are still based on ancient bead-making techniques. They can incorporate metallic foils or have surface decorations of molten glass.

Millefiori

Millefiori means 'thousand flowers'. These beautifully intricate Venetian glass beads are created from fine coloured glass rods which are bundled together in rows so that the cross-section of the bundle has a flower-like pattern. The glass is then reheated and stretched which fuses the rods together.

Plastic beads

Glass beads are often heavy and can weigh down a necklace. Plastic beads are a cheaper, lightweight alternative. They come in many sizes and finishes, such as metallic and pearlised effects. Mix a few plastic beads with glass or crystals to make your materials less expensive without compromising on a classy finish.

Crystals

Crystals are very striking as they twinkle in the light. They are available in lots of colours and faceted shapes – bicones, which have a diamond shaped profile and cubes are the most common shapes.

Seed beads

These small, inexpensive beads are usually sold by weight. They come in all the colours of the rainbow and range in size from 8/0 to 24/0. Confusingly, the larger the number, the smaller the bead.

Rocailles

Like seed beads, rocailles are usually sold by weight. These beads usually come with a square hole. Pearl effect rocailles are often called seed pearls, whereas short cylindrical versions are known as delicas or antiques.

Bugle beads

These versatile tubular glass beads are manufactured in lengths from 2–35 mm. They are great for stringing necklaces or adding embellishments and come in a sparkling multicoloured assortment.

Spacers

Spacers are beads, often metal, that are positioned between feature beads. They stop the feature beads from overpowering the look of the necklace and are often an inexpensive way of adding more beads.

Charms and pendants

Small decorative figures with a hole at the top for threading that can be hung singly on a pendant holder or jump ring from a chain or ribbon. Made from all sorts of materials – from acrylic, glass, resin, metal, shell and stone – charms add interest and a touch of individuality.

Drop beads

As the name suggests, these beads are in the shape of a drop and have a hole across the thinner end for threading. They can be hung on pendant holders or jump rings.

Pearls

These classic gems are found in sea and freshwater molluscs all over the world and have been popular for jewellery making since ancient Greek and Roman times. Cheap imitations, usually made of glass with a pearlised finish, are readily available in various sizes and subtle colours.

Semi-precious chips

An inexpensive way of using semi-precious gems is to buy them in chip form. Aquamarine, crystal and rose quartz are just a few of the varieties available.

Other materials

Consider unusual materials such as shells and feathers for adding special interest to necklaces. Whole shells or pieces of shell often come with drilled holes. Take care if drilling a hole yourself as shells are delicate and brittle, and can snap. Use a drill with a small bit when drilling and support the shell in a piece of plastic clay. If using feathers, secure the shaft in a tag end that can then be hung amongst a string of beads. Silk flowers are fun to take apart so that you can use the petals separately to turn into jewellery; see the Silk flower choker on pages 74–79.

Glass beads

Seed beads

Charms and pendants

Millefiori

Rocailles and bugle beads

Drop beads

Plastic beads

Pearls

Semi-precious chips

Crystals and bugle beads

Spacers

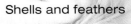

Shells and feathers

Threading material

Beads can be threaded and hung on many different materials. The size of hole in the bead will often determine the threading material. Thread beads with small holes on finer threads, such as Nymo. Large holed beads can be threaded onto cord or thong or fixed to them with pendant holders or head pins fixed to jump rings.

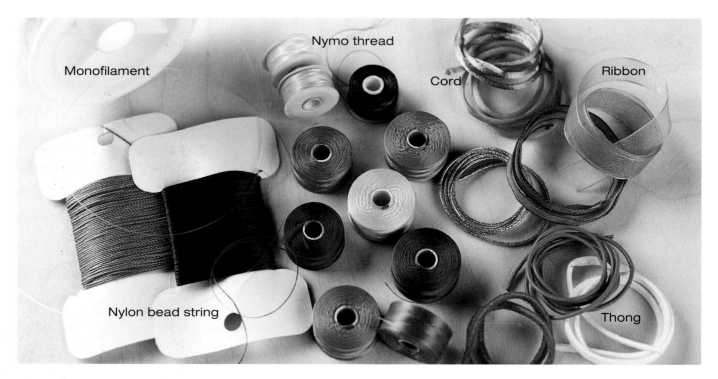

Nylon bead string

This strong non-stretch bead string comes in a range of colours and thicknesses. Size 2 is a suitable thickness for most applications. Thread or tie beads with large holes onto a size 8 bead string. Large beads will hang in a natural curve if the thread is knotted between each bead. The larger the size number, the thicker the string.

Nymo thread

This strong, multi-stranded nylon thread comes in different thicknesses and lots of lovely colours. Use Nymo thread for small beads and weaving techniques, such as the Daisy choker on pages 88–91.

Elastic cord

This is a stretchy, usually clear plastic material often used for stretch bracelets. It comes in light and heavy weights.

Nylon twist

This synthetic thread is best for small, lightweight beads. It is strong but prone to stretching.

Monofilament

This transparent thread is very strong and can be threaded without a needle. It is also available in black and a few translucent shades. Beads threaded on monofilament appear to float as the thread is almost invisible. Glue, tie or crimp beads to hold them in place.

Thong, cord and ribbon

Thong can be made of suede, leather, cotton or imitation skins in various thicknesses. Shiny round cord, which is often called rat tail, and cotton thong come in 1–3 mm ($1/24$–$1/8$ in) thicknesses and in many colours. Wide ribbon can be used to make chokers and narrow ribbon to fasten necklaces. Filmy organza ribbon gives a lovely, delicate look to jewellery.

Wire and chain

Wire comes in various thicknesses and materials. Specialist wire suppliers and bead shops always have a good selection to choose from. Gold-plated wire and nickel wire, which is a good substitute for pure silver wire, are the most widely available. Copper, brass, real gold, surgical steel and silver-plate are other alternatives. Coloured wire, made of coated copper alloy, is very appealing and fun to use.

Tiger tail

This very strong nylon-coated wire is available in different colours and thicknesses: 24 gauge is the most versatile thickness. Tiger tail can be threaded with sharp-edged beads which would fray thread and bead string. Use wire cutters to cut tiger tail and finish the ends with crimps when making necklaces. Store tiger tail in coils as it is difficult to straighten out any kinks that occur.

Chain

Chain can be bought by the metre or yard in various thicknesses, styles and finishes. Cut fine chain with wire snippers. To split a thick chain, use two pairs of pliers to pull a link open. Alternatively, you can make a home-made chain by linking jump rings together until you reach the length you require. Beads can be fixed to chain with jump rings or by threading them onto head pins, then passing the pin through a link in the chain and making a loop.

Beader's tip

The thickness or diameter of wire is measured in gauges. The higher the number, the thinner the wire. Forty gauge wire is the thinnest, and 10 gauge the thickest. Twenty-four gauge wire is used for many of the projects in this book as it is flexible but holds its shape. Knitting wire is available in pretty colours and is supplied on spools and, as the name suggests, is fine enough to knit or crochet with.

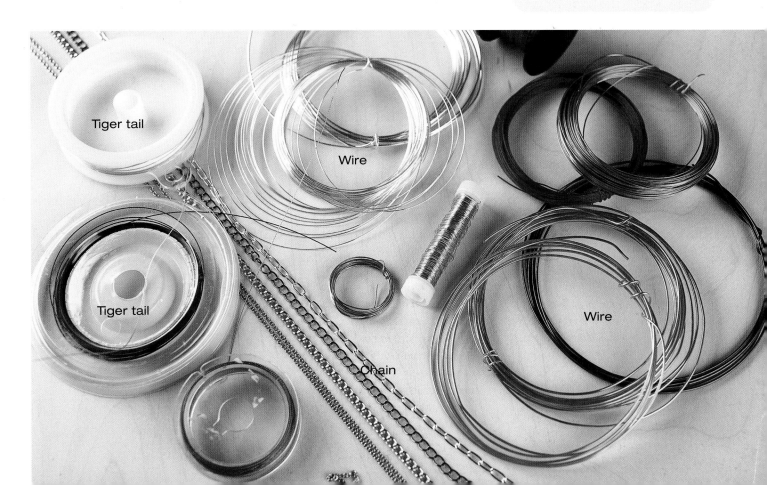

Tiger tail

Wire

Tiger tail

Chain

Wire

Findings

A broad term for manufactured components used to make a collection of beads into wearable jewellery. Usually made of metal, these include clasps, head and eye pins, jump rings, crimp beads and many more. Most findings are gold and silver but copper and black coated varieties are also available.

Head pins

Head pins resemble long dressmaking pins. They are available in a few different lengths, ranging from 2.5 cm (1 in) to 5.5 cm (2 1/4 in). 5.5-cm (2 1/4-in) head pins are the ones used most often in the projects in this book. A bead is threaded onto the pin and a loop made above the bead for hanging.

Eye pins

Eye pins have a loop (the eye) at one end. They are used for pinning beads or to tie the end of strings of beads to, the eye is then concealed in a bell cap. For pinning, a bead is threaded onto the pin and a loop made above it, ready to hook onto another pinned bead or a jump ring. You can make your own eye pins by turning a loop at the end of a length of 24-gauge wire, threading on a bead and making another loop above the bead.

Tag ends

These three-fold metal pieces anchor the ends of ribbon and cord. A ring at the top allows the tag to be fixed to a jump ring.

Jump rings

These small rings join components together and are used throughout the book. They are available in different sizes to join the loops of head pins, pendant holders and fastenings to necklaces. Oval jump rings are also available. Join a row of jump rings together to make a chain. See page 23 on a simple way to make jump rings.

Pendant holders or bails

The claws of a pendant holder or bail are squeezed onto the holes of a pendant or drop bead. Simple pendant holders are triangular; others are ornate and may have a ring at the top for hanging.

Spacer bars

Spacer bars have a row of drilled holes to thread beaded strings of beads through when making a multi-strand necklace or bracelet. They help the necklace hold its shape by separating the strings of beads.

End bars

Finish a multi-strand necklace with an end bar to match the style of the spacer bars.

Bell caps

Also known as end caps, you can hide the unsightly ends of tied multi-strand necklaces in them.

Crimps

These tiny metal cylinders finish the ends of tiger tail and wire necklaces neatly by concealing the end of the tiger tail or wire. They can also be used to separate beads on tiger tail or beading string. The crimps are secured in place with crimping pliers. Crimps can also be closed with snipe-nose pliers but the closed crimp will be flat and not as neat as the rounded shape crimping pliers produce.

Calottes

Necklaces strung on bead string or thread are finished with calottes, which consist of two hinged cups with a loop attached. The knotted thread ends are enclosed neatly and securely in the cups.

Necklace fastenings

Necklaces are fastened with all sorts of clasps and fastenings. Simple bolt rings fasten onto a jump ring or split ring, which resembles a small key ring. Barrel or torpedo clasps screw together. The tongue of a box-and-tongue clasp slots into the box. A toggle clasp fastens onto a ring as does a hook clasp.

Beader's tip

The terms 'gold' and 'silver' used in this book when referring to findings describes the colour of the metal only. It is not suggested you use precious metal. Most findings are made of base metal with a silver or gold plating, but many sterling silver and real gold findings are available from specialist jewellery-making suppliers if you prefer.

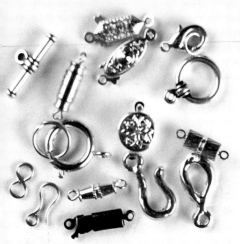

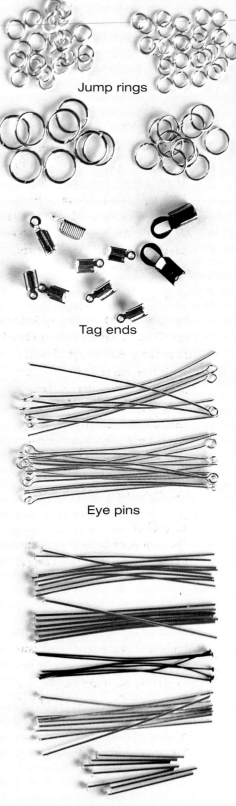

Jump rings

Bell caps

Necklace fastenings

Tag ends

End bars

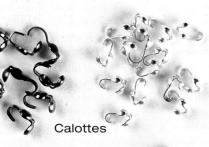

Calottes

Eye pins

Spacer bars

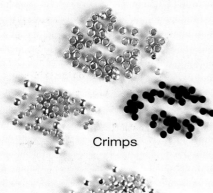

Crimps

Pendant holders

Head pins

Equipment

Only a few essential tools are needed to make the jewellery in this book. For comfort and safety, always work on a flat, clean, well lit surface and remember to keep sharp implements and glues beyond the reach of a child or pet.

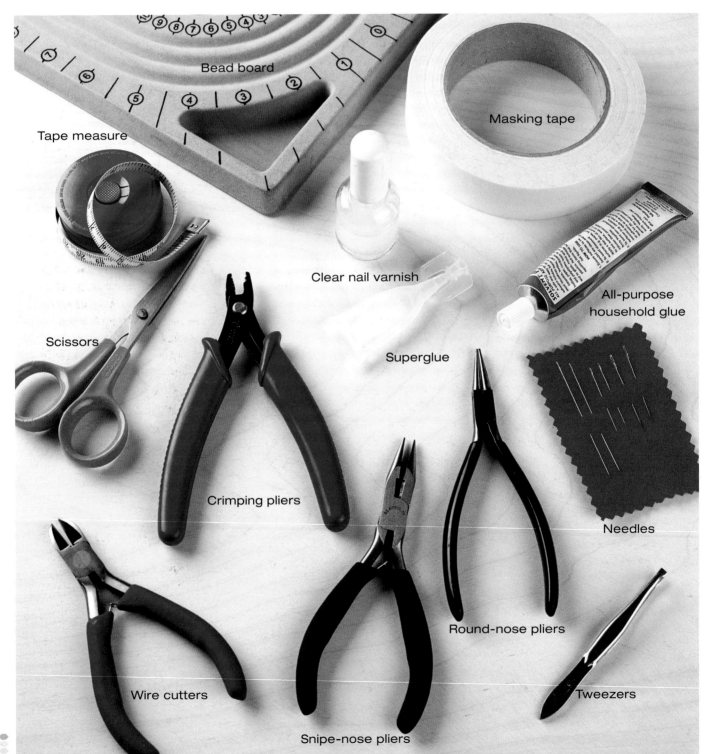

Bead board

Tape measure

Masking tape

Clear nail varnish

All-purpose household glue

Scissors

Superglue

Crimping pliers

Needles

Round-nose pliers

Wire cutters

Tweezers

Snipe-nose pliers

Tape measure

A flexible tape measure is useful when making necklaces. As a guide, a loose choker is 40 cm (16 in) long, a princess necklace is 45 cm (18 in) long and a matinée necklace is 52–63 cm (20–25 in) long. Longer necklaces don't need a fastener to open and close; you can fasten the ends with a knot then adjust the knot to hide it in a bead.

Wire cutters

Use wire cutters specifically for jewellery-making to snip wire and tiger tail as they are easier to get close to small components than the larger wire cutters used for DIY purposes.

Scissors

An old pair of scissors will suffice for fine wires but will blunt the blades in time. Use sharp embroidery scissors to cut threads, ribbon, thong, cord and fabric.

Snipe-nose pliers

These versatile pliers have flat faces and are used to close calottes, crimps and tag ends.

Round-nose pliers

These pliers are used to create loops. Additionally, jump rings can be opened or closed by holding one side of the ring with a pair of round-nose pliers and the other side with a pair of snipe-nose pliers.

Crimping pliers

These are used to secure crimps tightly and neatly. They have notches to hold the crimp and squeeze it closed. The crimp made with crimping pliers is more rounded than a crimp made with flat-nose pliers.

Tweezers

Tweezers come in handy to pick up tiny beads and for holding pieces in one hand while applying glue with the other.

Needles

Thread tiny beads such as rocailles with a beading needle. Traditionally, these are very long as the length makes them ideal for picking up a number of beads in one go. If you find the length difficult to handle, use a short beading needle instead. Size 10 is the most practical size – any larger and the needle may be too big for the bead hole, any smaller and the needles bend and break quickly.

Thicker threads for use with large beads will require a large needle: a size 7 is usually suitable. Needle sizes are graded in numbers: size 1 being the largest, and a diminutive size 16, the finest. Sew beads such as rocailles and bugles to ribbon and fabric with a size 10 crewel embroidery needle.

Superglue

A small dab of superglue will secure knots. Use a tube or bottle with a fine nozzle for a controlled application. Superglue should be stored upright to prevent the nozzle from getting clogged.

Clear nail varnish

Is suitable for gluing knots and sealing the ends of woven cord and ribbon to prevent fraying. Alternatively, dab the ends of cord or ribbon with all-purpose household glue to prevent them fraying whilst you are threading.

Masking tape

This low-tack adhesive tape can be wrapped around the end of tiger tail or wire to stop beads slipping off the end whilst you are working.

Bead board

A useful addition to your toolbox, a bead board has a non-slip surface and a U-shaped graded groove to arrange beads in when designing a necklace. Alternatively, arrange the beads on a

towel, piece of fleece or felt so that they do not roll away. Choose a white or skin-toned surface, as a strong colour will affect the appearance of your design and the colours you use.

Storage

Be warned, beads get everywhere! Small beads are often supplied in seal-top bags or plastic cylinders with plug-in lids. These containers are good for storage as they do not take up much space and are transparent for easy identification. Clear stubby cylinders with screw-on lids are widely available. They are ideal for storing beads and are easily accessible when beading as the wide opening means you can slip a needle through the mass of beads to pick them up.

Beader's tip

Tip larger beads into shallow bowls and saucers when working but keep them in sealed containers at other times to protect them from dust. Store all beads away from direct sunlight as colours may fade with long exposure to bright light.

Techniques

Before embarking on a project, read the instructions carefully to check that you are familiar with the techniques used. All the techniques described here have been used throughout the book. Always follow metric or imperial measurements, but not a combination of both.

Making a necklace

If you are using a selection of beads, arrange them on a bead board or non-slip surface to see if you are happy with the design. Work outwards from the centre when arranging the beads, that way, you can work symmetrically (if that is your plan) and you will also be able to concentrate the most interesting part of the design towards the front.

Threading beads

Beads can be threaded onto a variety of stringing materials. Tiger tail is used here; it is strong enough for heavy beads and holds its shape well. If you work with the stringing material laid in a curve, you will get a good idea of the finished look.

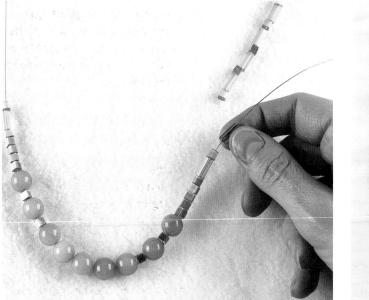

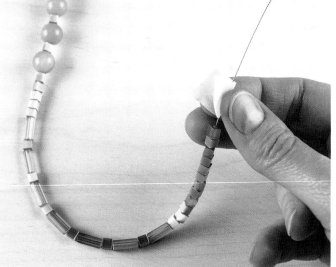

1 Snip a length of tiger tail 25 cm (10 in) longer than the intended length of the necklace. This will allow extra tiger tail for adjusting the length and fixing to jump rings. Thread beads onto the tiger tail, working outwards from both sides of the centre. If you are only using one type of bead or alternating beads, they can be threaded from one end.

2 To prevent beads slipping off the end of the wire, wrap a piece of masking tape around one end. Working outwards from the centre allows for beads to be added or taken away from the length of the necklace. Remove the tape when you are ready to finish the ends of the tiger tail with your choice of findings.

Fixing crimps

Crimps resemble small, round metal beads. They are quick to apply and give a professional finish to a necklace. Crimps are best fixed with crimping pliers but snipe nose pliers will suffice.

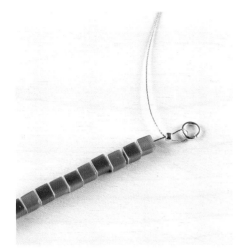

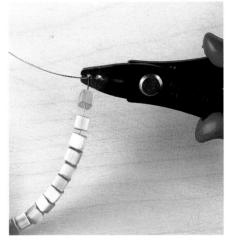

1 Slip one crimp then one jump ring onto one end of the tiger tail. Pull the end of the tiger tail back through the crimp until the crimp sits 4 mm ($^5/_{32}$ in) from the last bead and the jump ring 4 mm ($^5/_{32}$ in) from the crimp.

2 Place the crimp in the inner notch of a pair of crimping pliers. Squeeze the pliers closed. The squashed crimp will be crescent shaped.

3 Next, place the crimp in the outer notch of the crimping pliers. Squeeze the pliers closed. This will round the shape of the crimp. If necessary, turn the crimp in the notch and close the pliers again to improve the shape. Snip off the excess wire as close as possible to the crimp. Repeat at the other end of the necklace.

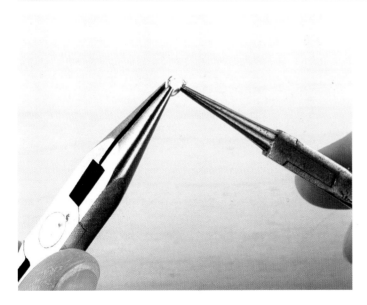

Using jump rings

Jump rings are used throughout the projects. Using two pairs of pliers, it is important to open and close the jump ring sideways. Do not pull the jump ring open outwards as it will weaken and may snap.

1 Hold the jump ring with a pair of pliers on one side of the opening and another pair of pliers on the other side of the opening, for example, use a pair of snipe-nose and a pair of round-nose pliers. Open the jump ring by gently pulling one pair of pliers up towards you until the opening is large enough to slip your jewellery component onto.

Fixing a necklace clasp

There are many different styles of clasp, choose one to suit your beads. An intricate vintage looking clasp would look good with a traditional necklace, and a more contemporary clasp with a vibrant modern style. Also consider the size; use a small clasp on a necklace of delicate beads and a chunky clasp with larger beads.

1 Open the jump ring at each end of the necklace. Slip the loop of each half of your chosen necklace clasp onto the jump ring and close it securely. If one half of the necklace fastens with a ring, slip the ring onto the jump ring.

2 Slip the jump ring through the hole or loop of the component then close the jump ring in the same way, aligning the join. Secure the join with a dab of superglue or clear nail varnish if you wish.

Stop beads

When threading beads on thread, start with a stop bead to prevent the beads from slipping off the end. Use a bead contrasting in colour to the necklace beads, then you won't forget to remove it!

1 Thread the stop bead onto the thread, then insert the needle through the bead again, leaving a trailing end of thread about 25 cm (10 in) long. Pull off the stop bead when the beading is completed. Use the trailing end to finish the necklace.

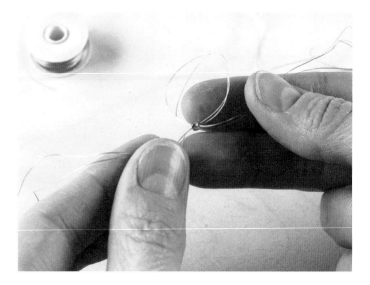

Wiring beads with fine wire

This technique is great fun to experiment with and quite elaborate designs can be achieved by threading lightweight beads and twisting the fine wire. Use knitting wire for lightweight beads and gauge 24 wire for heavier beads. See the Twisted wire necklace on pages 54–59 and the Wired flower necklace on pages 122–127.

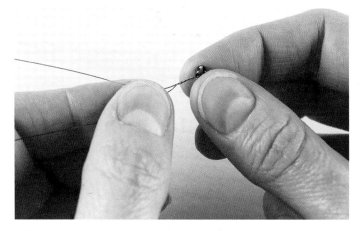

1 To start, thread a bead onto knitting wire (as a guide, snip the wire three times the length of the finished piece) and adjust it to sit in the centre of the wire. Twist both ends of the wire together for 5 mm ($^1/_4$ in) to secure the bead in place. You now have two wires which will be called the first and second wire.

2 Slip another bead onto the first wire and hold it 1 cm ($^3/_8$ in) from the last twist. Twist the first wire on itself until you reach the second wire. Repeat on the second wire. Continue adding beads to the wire in this way.

Making jump rings

This is a fast and novel way to make your own jump rings. It is especially useful when using coloured wire if coloured findings are not available. Gauges 20 and 24 are suitable sizes; finer wire will not hold its shape.

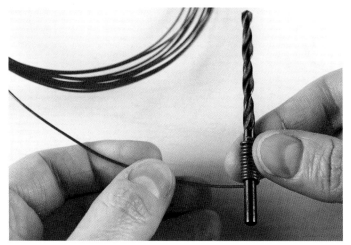

1 Bind the wire tightly around a suitable straight metal mould. A drill bit is ideal: the diameter of the drill bit will be the inner size of the jump ring.

2 Pull the coiled wire off the drill bit. Snip through the coils with wire cutters.

Using head pins

Head pins are useful for threading beads onto to hang from a necklace. The most common lengths are 2.5 cm (1 in) and 5.5 cm (2¹/₄ in).

1 Thread the bead or a selection of beads onto a head pin. Start with a small bead if the other bead holes are large and prone to slip off the head of the head pin. Cut off the excess wire, leaving 8 mm (⁵/₁₆ in) above the last bead.

2 Hold the head pin with a pair of round-nose pliers 3 mm (¹/₈ in) from the tips of the jaws, bend the wire into a loop towards you as you form it so that it is centred over the last bead.

Making pinned beads

If you will be making a number of pinned beads, wrap a narrow strip of masking tape around one of the jaws of the round-nose pliers to mark the place to hold the eye pin when making the loop. This will ensure that all the loops will be the same size.

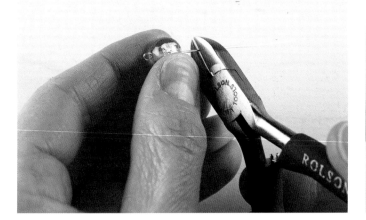

1 Thread the bead or a selection of beads onto an eye pin. Cut off the excess wire, leaving 8 mm (⁵/₁₆ in) above the last bead.

2 With round-nose pliers resting against the last bead, bend the wire into a loop towards you as you form it so that it is centred over the last bead. To attach pinned beads together, use round-nose pliers to open a loop on one bead sideways, slip onto the loop of another bead, then close the first loop.

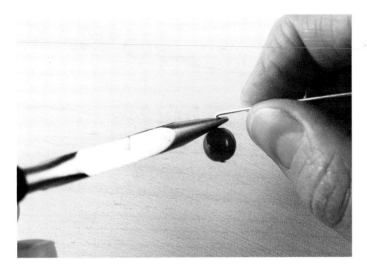

Making wrapped loops

A wrapped loop gives extra strength on a head pin or pinned bead. Bear in mind that a wrapped loop cannot be opened so if pinning beads, fix a jump ring between the pinned beads.

1 Thread the bead or a selection of beads onto a head pin or an eye pin. Cut off the excess wire, leaving 4 cm (1½ in) above the last bead. Hold the wire with a pair of snipe-nose pliers, resting the jaws on the last bead. Using your fingers, bend the wire over the jaws at a right angle.

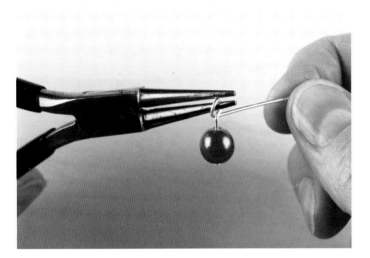

2 Make a loop above the bend in the wire using a pair of round-nose pliers, ending up with the wire again at right angles to the wire coming from the bead.

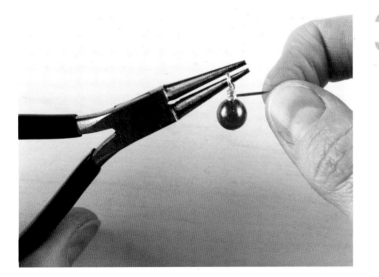

3 With the round-nose pliers slipped through the loop to hold the pin steady, wrap the extending wire neatly around the wire coming from the bead. Snip off the excess wire close to the bead. Squeeze the snipped end close to the wrapped wire with a pair of snipe-nose pliers.

Fixing a pendant holder

Consider the direction that the pendant will face. Some pendant holders have a loop at the top. A jump ring can be fixed to the pendant holder to face it in a different direction or to lengthen the drop of the pendant.

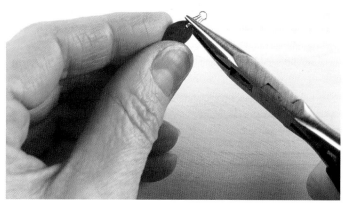

1 Gently tease the claws of a pendant holder open until the gap between the claws is large enough to slip your component onto one claw. Slip a drop bead, charm or pendant onto one claw.

2 Squeeze the pendant holder closed with a pair of snipe-nose pliers.

Hanging beads

Beads can be hung on head pins or pendant holders, but a long length of hanging beads can hang on thread; this gives a softer look as the beads will sway on the thread. Use this technique to attach a fringe or single length of hanging beads to a ribbon or to a beaded necklace. You can work with a single or double length of thread; a double length will naturally be stronger.

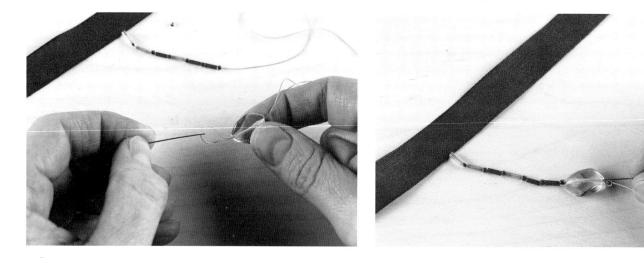

1 If hanging beads from a ribbon, sew the thread to the ribbon a few times to secure it. Thread the beads onto the thread to the desired length.

2 Insert the needle back through all the beads except the last one and pull the thread so the beads lay end to end. Fasten the thread to the ribbon or continue making the necklace.

Fixing a tag end

Threading material that is too thick to fix in a calotte can be finished with a tag end instead which neatly encloses the end of a thong, cord or ribbon.

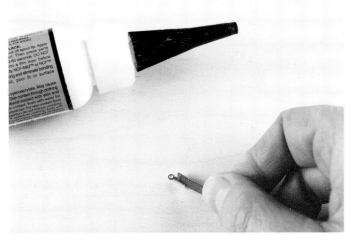

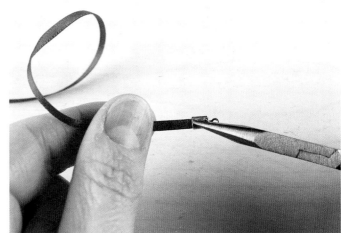

1   Glue the end of a thong, cord or ribbon in the centre of a tag end with superglue.

2   Fold one side of the tag over the centre with a pair of snipe-nose pliers. Fold over the other side of the tag end with the pliers. Squeeze the tag end tightly closed with the pliers.

Fixing calottes

The ends of necklaces strung on thread are secured in calottes, which are then fixed on jump rings to the necklace clasp. Calottes give a neat, professional finish as they hide the raw ends of the thread and stop the ends from fraying.

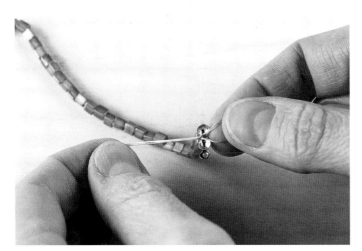

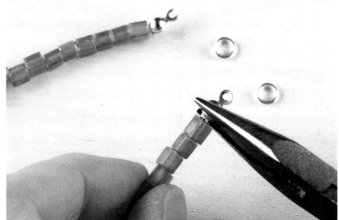

1   Insert the thread at one end of a necklace through the hole in a calotte. Tie the thread in a large knot and cut off the excess thread. Glue the knot in one cup of the calotte with superglue.

2   Squeeze the cups closed with a pair of snipe-nose pliers. Slip the loop of the calotte onto a jump ring. Repeat at the other end of the necklace.

THE projects

Floating glass star necklace

Floating glass star necklace

Four strands of monofilament, which is a clear nylon line, are threaded with crystal stars to make this pretty necklace. Monofilament is transparent so the stars appear to float.

Materials and tools

320 cm (3½ yd) of 0.4-mm (¹⁄₁₆-in) monofilament

44 crystal star-shaped glass beads

Masking tape

2 silver calottes

2 x 5-mm (¼-in) silver jump rings

Silver torpedo necklace clasp

Superglue

Embroidery scissors

Snipe-nose pliers

1 Cut four 80-cm (31¹⁄₂-in) lengths of monofilament. Thread a star bead onto one length.

2 To secure the star 8 cm (3¹⁄₄ in) from one end of the monofilament, fold the leading end of the monofilament over the star and insert it through the star again. Pull the monofilament to anchor the star.

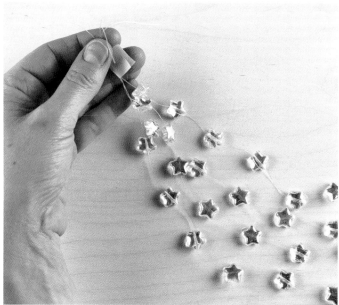

3 Repeat to secure eleven stars to each length of monofilament, 2.5 cm (1 in) apart.

4 Lay the strands on your work surface in a curve. Adjust the stars to sit between one another, so that the inner strand is shorter, graduating to a longer outer strand. Stick a piece of masking tape around the strands at each end of the necklace to hold all the strands in the correct position.

Beader's tip

Hold up the necklace when the ends are taped to check that it hangs in a pleasing curve. If necessary, adjust the strands before fixing the calottes.

5 Refer to the Fixing calottes technique on page 27 to finish the necklace with calottes and a torpedo clasp. Remove the masking tape.

▲ Multi-coloured floating necklace

Here, three strands of monofilament have multi-coloured beads positioned at irregular intervals. Five 25-cm (10-in) lengths of monofilament are tied at their centres to each strand between the front beads. Beads are then fastened to the extending lengths of monofilament and beads knotted to the ends. A dab of superglue on the knots secures the end beads in place.

▼ Red floating necklace

Here is a striking necklace that is very quick to make. Seventeen red glass cube beads are placed 5 mm ($1/4$ in) apart on a single strand of monofilament.

▲ Green floating necklace

This floating necklace has assorted green glass and plastic beads secured at irregular intervals along two strands of monofilament. The necklace fastens with a bolt ring fastening.

▼ Turquoise floating necklace

Three strands of monofilament are dotted with plastic turquoise beads in various sizes positioned 1.5 cm ($5/8$ in) apart.

Antique jewellery necklace

Antique jewellery necklace

It is always worth saving beads from a piece of broken jewellery, even if only a few are reusable. Here is a super way to recycle your favourite beads to great effect. Hang them between a chain, some pretty pinned beads and leaf sprig-shaped charms with a hole at each end.

Materials and tools

8 silver eye pins

9 x 5-mm (1/4-in) red glass cube beads

1 x 5.5-cm (2 1/4-in) silver head pin

8 silver leaf sprig shaped charms with a hole at each end

1 x 2 cm (3/4 in) silver heart charm

2 silver triangular pendant holders

1.2 cm (1/2 in) silver butterfly shaped bead

22 cm (8 1/2 in) tiger tail

2 silver crimps

Assorted glass, metal and ceramic beads, ranging from 1 cm (3/8 in) to 2.5 cm (1 in) in diameter

4 x 5 mm (1/4 in) silver jump rings

27 cm (10 1/2 in) silver chain

1 silver box-and-tongue necklace clasp

Wire cutters

Round-nose pliers

Snipe-nose pliers

Crimping pliers

1 Follow the Making pinned beads technique on page 24 to make eight pinned beads using the eye pins and eight of the red glass cube beads. Fix each pinned bead to the lower hole of a leaf sprig shaped charm.

2 Fix one of the pinned beads to the top hole of one of the other leaf sprig shaped charms. Hang a silver heart charm to the lower pinned cube bead. Fix a triangular pendant holder to the top hole of the top leaf sprig shaped charm.

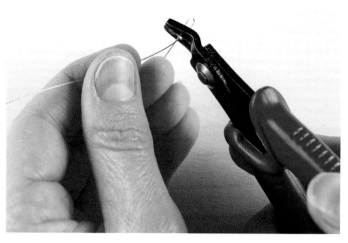

3 Thread the butterfly shaped bead then the remaining red glass cube bead onto a head pin. Snip the wire and make a loop at the top following the Using head pins technique on page 24. Fix a triangular pendant holder to the loop.

4 Thread a crimp onto one end of the tiger tail and pull the wire back through the crimp. Adjust the loop of the tiger tail to sit 5 mm ($1/4$ in) from the crimp. Secure the crimp with crimping pliers, then snip off the excess wire.

Beader's tip

Even just a few antique beads will be very effective. Simply add a longer length chain at each end of the necklace if using fewer beads.

5 Thread on the beads and the pendant holders of the heart and butterfly until the width of the threaded beads is 13.5 cm ($5^1/4$ in).

6 Thread a crimp onto the tiger tail and pull the end of the tiger tail back through the crimp. Adjust the crimp to sit 5 mm ($^1/_4$ in) after the last bead and the loop of the tiger tail 5 mm ($^1/_4$ in) from the crimp. Secure the crimp with crimping pliers and snip off the excess wire.

7 Join the remaining leaf sprig shaped charms and pinned cube beads together in two lengths of three leaf charms and cube beads. Open the loop under the lower pinned cube bead and slip it through the end loops of the tiger tail. Close the loops with round- and snipe-nose pliers.

8 Snip the chain in half with wire cutters. Slip a jump ring through the top hole of each top leaf sprig shaped charm. Slip the end link of each chain onto the jump rings, then close the jump rings with a pair of round-nose pliers and a pair of snipe-nose pliers.

9 Slip a jump ring through the link at the other end of the chain. Slip the jump rings through the rings of a box-and-tongue necklace clasp, then close the jump rings with the pliers.

◄ Smokey glass antique necklace

Black wire, chain and findings are used to give this dramatic necklace an antique look. A purple glass teardrop bead is fixed to a head pin with a wrapped loop and hangs on a length of five pinned glass beads on black wire with a wrapped loop at each end to make a stunning pendant. The pendant hangs between glass and metal beads and rocaille beads threaded on tiger tail. The tiger tail hangs between black chains and fastens with a simple lobster claw necklace fastening.

▸ Velvet ribbon antique necklace

A velvet ribbon is used in place of chain on this necklace of chunky glass and crystal beads. Diamante spacers are placed between the beads to lengthen the strand. The tiger tail is fixed between two-hole end bars sewn to the ribbon which fastens with a fabulous antique jewelled fastening.

◂ Fine chain antique necklace

The centrepiece of this delicate necklace is a pinned turquoise millefiori glass bead which hangs between two chains. The chains have three pinned crystals and a glass bead between the links each side of the centre. A pinned metal rose shaped bead hangs from the pinned millefiori bead and suspends two lengths of pinned glass beads and crystals between short lengths of chain with single beads on head pins at the ends.

◂ Copper and pearl antique necklace

Instead of using chains, these glass and metal copper coloured beads hang between lengths of pale copper coloured potato shaped pearls. The beads and pearls are threaded onto tiger tail and finished with crimps. Copper leaf sprig shaped charms with a hole at each end joins the lengths of tiger tail. The necklace is fastened with a copper box-and-tongue necklace clasp.

Twisted necklace

Twisted necklace

This fabulous necklace has four strands of beads of different textures and sizes in pretty shades of turquoise. Delicate twig shaped charms suspend berry-like freshwater pearls. Twist the strands of the necklace together before wearing to create a swirl of beads. The tighter the twist, the shorter the necklace.

Materials and tools

25 g (1 oz) size 11 pale blue rocaille beads

Approx. 122 baroque turquoise freshwater pearls

7 x 2.5-cm (1-in) silver head pins

7 silver twig shaped charms with a hole at each end

Pale blue Nymo thread

26 x 1.2-cm ($^1/_2$-in) long flat oval pale blue glass beads

Approx. 98 x 4-mm ($^1/_4$-in) pale grey fibre optic cube beads

50 g (2 oz) of blue topaz dyed chips

2 silver eye pins

Superglue

2 x 8-mm ($^5/_{32}$-in) diameter silver bell caps

2 x 4-mm ($^1/_4$-in) silver jump rings

Silver toggle necklace clasp

Round-nose pliers

Snipe-nose pliers

Wire cutters

4 size 10 beading needles

4 beads to use as stop beads

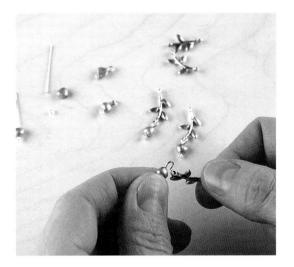

1 Thread one rocaille bead then a freshwater pearl onto each head pin. Make a loop at the top following the Using head pins technique on page 24. Open the loop and slip it onto the bottom hole of each twig charm. Close the loop with a pair of round- and snipe-nose pliers.

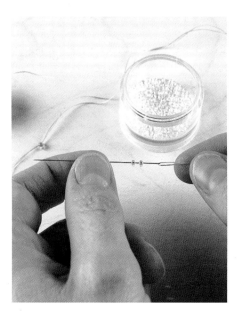

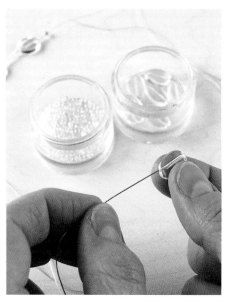

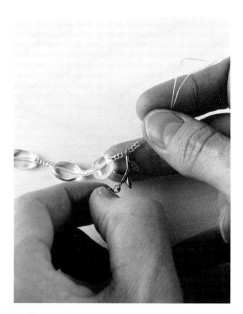

2 Thread each needle with a 105-cm (41 1/2-in) double length of thread. Attach a stop bead to the end of each length, leaving a 25-cm (10-in) trailing end of thread. Thread on two pale blue rocaille beads.

3 Thread on one flat oval bead. Thread on a sequence of six rocaille beads then one flat oval bead, three times.

4 Thread on three rocaille beads, one twig charm and three rocaille beads.

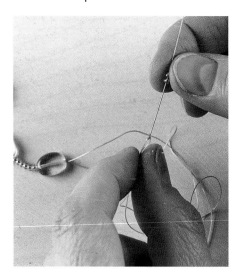

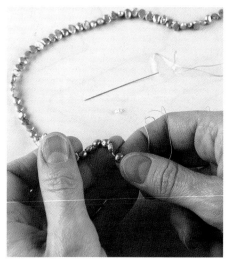

5 Repeat Steps 2 and 3 six times. Thread on one flat oval bead. Thread on two rocaille beads.

6 Repeat Step 2 on the next thread. Thread on one fibre optic cube bead and one rocaille bead. Continue alternating one cube bead and one rocaille bead and finally add two rocaille beads until the beads are the same length as the previous strand.

7 Thread a stop bead and two rocaille beads on the next thread. Thread on freshwater pearls and finally add two rocaille beads until the beaded strand is the same length as the previous strands.

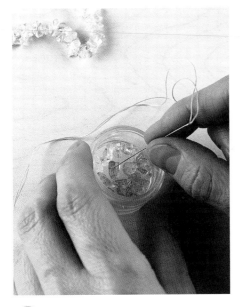

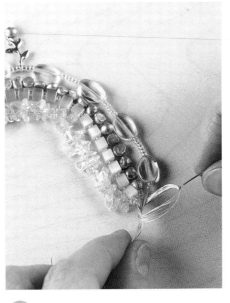

8 Thread a stop bead and two rocaille beads on the next thread. Thread on blue topaz dyed chips and finally add two rocaille beads until the beaded strand is the same length as the previous strands.

9 Holding all the threads together, tie extending ends of thread to the eye of an eye pin with a double knot, pulling the threads tight so that they hang close to the loop of the eye pin.

10 Insert each needle back through the last eight beads of each strand. Dab the knot with superglue, then cut off the excess thread close to the beads.

11 Remove the stop beads at the other ends of the strands. Holding all the threads together, tie the extending ends of threads to the eye of an eye pin with a double knot, as in Step 9. Thread two thread ends onto a needle. Insert the needle through the last eight beads of one strand. Repeat with the remaining thread ends through the other strands of beads. Dab the knot with superglue, then cut off the excess thread close to the beads.

12 Insert each eye pin through a bell cap. Thread on two rocaille beads. Snip the wire 8 mm ($5/16$ in) above the last rocaille bead. Make a loop with the round-nose pliers and fix a jump ring to each loop. Finally, fix the necklace clasp to the jump rings.

◄ Purple and blue twisted necklace

Vibrant purple and blue miracle beads are dotted along four strands of purple elastic on this lively necklace. To secure each bead, thread it onto elastic, fold the leading end of the elastic back over the bead and insert it through the bead again. Pull the elastic to anchor the bead in place. Each end of the elastic has a jump ring threaded on and the end crimped. The four jump rings at each end of the necklace are then slipped onto a single jump ring and fixed to a barrel necklace clasp.

▼ Green twisted necklace

A few handmade glass beads are interspersed along one strand of this brightly coloured necklace of five strands of lime green rocaille beads.

▶ Glass and ceramic twisted necklace

This bold necklace has one strand of brown glass triangular beads, one strand of black ceramic triangular beads and one strand of 3-mm ($^1/_8$-in) diameter blue glass beads. The over sized bolt ring fastening suits the scale of the twisted strands.

Beader's tip

This necklace also looks great worn untwisted, which would make it a longer length.

◀ Copper twisted necklace

Here is a regal necklace of three strands of rich copper coloured beads. One strand has a sequence alternating nine goldstone chips and three 5mm ($^1/_4$ in) metallic beads. Another strand has size 9 metal rocaille beads interspersed with six arrow shaped charms. The other strand alternates a sequence of five size 7 metallic rocaille beads and one 5mm ($^1/_4$ in) glass bead.

Peyote tube necklace

Peyote tube necklace

This elegant necklace is created with a traditional peyote bead weaving technique that creates a tube of beads in a brickwork pattern. A ring of nine beads determines the circumference of the tube but any odd number of beads can be used, although the necklace will not hang neatly if you use more than 13 beads in a ring.

Materials and tools

Matching Nymo thread

50 g (2 oz) size 11 red glass rocaille beads

2 x 8-mm ($^5/_{32}$-in) diameter silver bell caps

2 silver eye pins

Superglue

2 x 5-mm ($^1/_4$-in) silver jump rings

Silver box-and-tongue necklace clasp

Size 10 beading needle

Embroidery scissors

Wire cutters

Round-nose pliers

Snipe-nose pliers

1 Thread the needle with a 2-m (2$^1/_4$-yd) double length of thread. Thread nine rocaille beads onto the thread. Tie the thread in a knot, leaving a 15-cm (6-in) tail of thread. You now have a ring of beads.

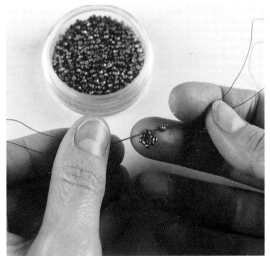

2 Hold the ring of beads steady by slipping the tail end of thread between the fingers of your supporting hand. Working in a clockwise direction, insert the needle back through the first bead and thread on a bead.

3 Insert the needle through the third bead of the ring, then thread on another bead.

4 Continue threading on beads in this way, adding a new bead between every other bead of the ring.

5 Pull the thread tight, the strung beads will begin to form a tube. Continue until the tube is 38 cm (15 in) long.

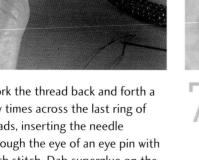

6 Work the thread back and forth a few times across the last ring of beads, inserting the needle through the eye of an eye pin with each stitch. Dab superglue on the fastening. Insert the needle back through the last few beads then cut off the excess thread.

7 Insert the eye pin through a bell cap. Snip the wire 8 mm ($5/16$ in) above the bell cap. Use a pair of round-nose pliers to make a loop. Fix a jump ring to the loop.

8 Thread the tail of thread at the start of the necklace on a needle. Repeat Steps 5 to 6. Finally, fix the necklace clasp to the jump rings.

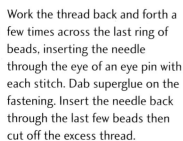
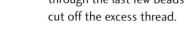

▲ Gold peyote necklace

This smart necklace of two shades of gold metal beads looks like an expensive, dense chain necklace. The different shades of gold give a lovely antique look to this necklace.

▲ Orange peyote necklace

Here is a chunky collar using two shades of orange beads and a ring of thirteen beads. It is made using the same techniques as for the main project. The cylindrical shape rocailles used here give a different look to that of the rondel shape rocaille beads used in the main project.

▲ Black and silver chain necklace

Create elegant stripes by working a ring of nine beads in a sequence of two black beads and one silver bead three times. If you are daunted by making an entire necklace, this short length hanging on fine chain may be the answer. This peyote tube is 9 cm (3 1/2 in) long.

▼ Peyote thong necklace

Start with a ring of 13 blue beads to make these hooped peyote stitch beads. Continue with another 13 blue beads, 26 green beads, 26 blue beads, 26 green beads and 26 blue beads. Weave the extending thread back through the beads. The three peyote stitch beads are threaded onto a 50-cm (20-in) length of lime green thong with lime green pony beads between them. A tag end and jump ring are fixed to each end with a barrel necklace clasp fastening.

Beader's tip

You will run out of thread a few times when working the peyote stitch. When the thread starts to get short, insert the needle back through the tube, inserting the needle in and out of the beads. Cut off the excess thread close to the tube. Thread the needle with a new long, double length of thread. Working in a clockwise direction, insert the needle in and out of the last few two rows of beads to secure the thread in place and bring the needle out through the last bead. Continue making the tube.

Glass lariat

This vibrant lariat is very simple to make. A lariat is a versatile length of beading that can be worn in many ways. Bend it in half and pull the ends through the loop or wrap it twice around your neck and loosely knot the ends at the front. This lariat is 140 cm (55 in) long.

Materials and tools

Turquoise size 8 nylon bead string

Approx. 23 multicoloured 1.5 cm–2.5 cm (^{5}/8–1 in) glass beads

Approx. 30 x 3-mm (^{1}/8-in) pale orange and purple pearl beads

Approx. 30 x 6-mm (^{1}/4-in) purple, cerise and pink pearl beads

Approx. 16 x 4-mm (^{1}/4-in) lime green cube plastic beads

Approx. 12 x 8-mm (^{5}/32-in) two-tone pink and turquoise plastic beads

Superglue

Size 7 embroidery needle

Embroidery scissors

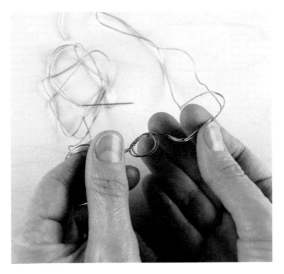

1 Thread a needle with a 2-m (1^1/4-yd) double length of nylon bead string. Tie a knot 20 cm (8 in) from the end. Tie another knot 3 cm (1^1/4 in) from the first knot.

2 Thread on a 3-mm (^{1}/8-in) pearl bead, an 8-mm (^{5}/32-in) plastic bead, a large glass bead, a 6-mm (^{1}/4in) pearl bead and a 3-mm (^{1}/8-in) pearl bead. Tie a knot after the last bead.

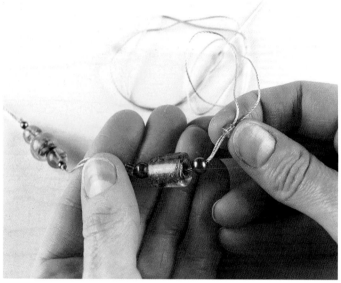

3 Tie a knot 3 cm (1¼ in) from the last bead. Continue this beading sequence of two smaller beads each side of a larger bead. Leave a gap of 3 cm (1¼ in) between the knots. Occasionally thread on a small bead, an 8-mm (⁵/₃₂-in) plastic bead and a 3-mm (¹/₈-in) pearl bead. Make the last knot approximately 20 cm (8 in) from the end of the thread.

4 Thread on a cube bead, an 8-mm (⁵/₃₂-in) plastic bead, a large glass bead, an 8-mm (⁵/₃₂-in) plastic bead and finally a cube bead.

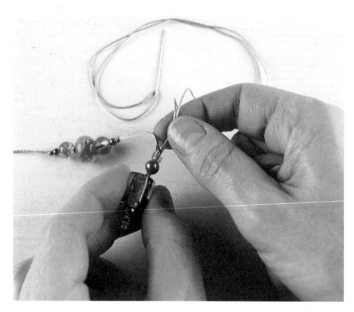

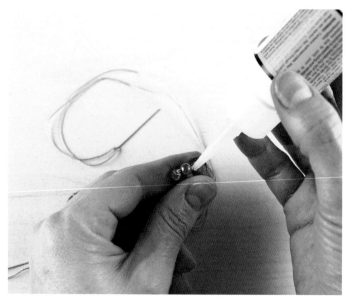

5 Missing the last cube bead, insert the needle through the last sequence of beads and pull the thread tight.

6 Part the glass bead and one of the 6-mm (¹/₄-in) pearl beads. Dab the thread with superglue between the beads. Cut off the excess thread close to the beads. Repeat at the other end of the lariat.

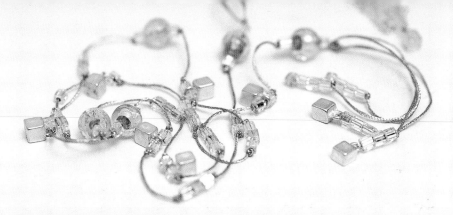

▲ Green and silver lariat

Lime green and silver beads and charms are threaded on silver embroidery thread on this metallic lariat. The knots are 2.5 cm (1 in) apart. The ends are finished with long, elegant tassels.

To add a tassel, after the last knot on the lariat, thread on a 5-mm (^{1}/$_4$-in) silver cube bead, a 1.2-cm (^{1}/$_2$-in) lime green and silver round bead and another 5-mm (^{1}/$_4$-in) silver cube bead. Insert the needle back through the beads but do not pull the thread tight yet. Slip two 40-cm (16-in) lengths of thread through the loop. Now pull the thread tight and glue in place. Knot the hanging threads together at the centre. Thread three 5-mm (^{1}/$_4$-in) silver cube beads onto each end. Thread a 4-mm (^{1}/$_4$-in) lime green cube plastic bead onto two ends of thread. Thread a 5-mm (^{1}/$_4$-in) silver cube charm bead onto the other two ends. Insert the needle back through the silver beads and pull the thread tight. Part two beads, dab with glue and cut off the excess thread.

▲ Lilac and blue lariat

This lariat of cool blue, lilac and purple beads is threaded on a single length of lilac silk bead cord and the knots are 2 cm (^{3}/$_4$ in) apart. Blue drop beads fixed to pendant holders are also tied to the lariat.

▲ Pink lariat

Instead of coloured bead string, this pretty lariat is threaded on a fine nylon thread. Rocaille beads in shades of pink are threaded between the larger pink and yellow glass and pearl beads.

Beader's tip

Use the point of a blunt needle, such as a tapestry needle, to guide the knot of the thread when positioning it.

▶ Coin necklace

This delicate, ethnic necklace of assorted beads and golden coins tied on a cream nylon bead string fastens with calottes and a box-and-tongue necklace clasp. The necklace is 43 cm (17 in) long. A short length of bead string is tied to the centre of the necklace with more beads and coins tied on. The ends of the centre string are finished in the same way as the main project with a coin instead of a cube bead on the ends.

Twisted wire necklace

Twisted wire necklace

This quirky necklace of 'branches' of subtly coloured beads is created by twisting coloured wire to secure the beads in place. The wire is easy to bend into shape to make the beads stand proud of the necklace.

Materials and tools

Approx. 112 assorted freshwater pearls, coloured crystal, silver and glass beads, ranging from 3 mm ($^1/_8$ in) to 8 mm ($^5/_{32}$ in) in diameter

Red knitting wire

2 silver crimps

2 x 4-mm ($^1/_6$-in silver) jump rings

1 silver bolt ring necklace clasp

Wire cutters

Crimping pliers

Round-nose pliers

Snipe-nose pliers

1 Snip one 120-cm (47-in) length of wire. Thread one bead onto the centre of the wire. Bring the wires together under the bead and twist them together for 5-mm ($^1/_4$-in) to secure the bead at the centre. You now have two wires extending which will be referred to as the first and second wire.

2 Thread a bead onto the first wire. Hold the bead 5-mm ($^1/_4$-in) along the wire. Twist the first wire on itself under the bead until you reach the second wire.

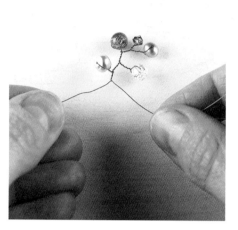

3 Twist both wires together for 5 mm (¹/₄ in).

4 Thread a bead onto the second wire. Hold the bead 5 mm (¹/₄ in) along the wire. Twist the second wire on itself under the bead until you reach the first wire.

5 Twist both wires together for 5 mm (¹/₄ in). Repeat Step 2 to 4 until you have five beads on the wires. This will be the centre branch. Twist both wires together for 5 mm (¹/₄ in), then splay the wires open.

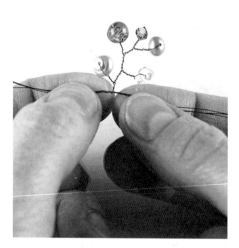

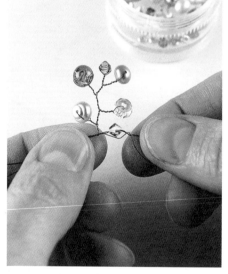

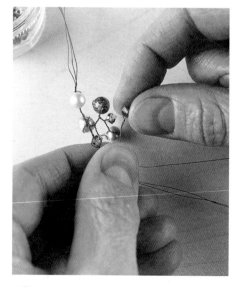

6 Snip two 120-cm (47-in) lengths of wire. Match the centre of the wires to the centre branch of the twisted wire. Twist the three wires together for 3 mm (¹/₈ in) each side of the centre branch.

7 Thread a bead onto the two longest wires on one side of the centre branch. Twist the three wires together for 3 mm (¹/₈ in) to secure the bead. Repeat on the other side of the centre branch.

8 To make a short branch, thread a bead onto one of the longest wires on one side of the centre branch. Hold the bead 2 cm (³/₄ in) along the wire. Twist the wire on itself under the bead for 5 mm (¹/₄ in).

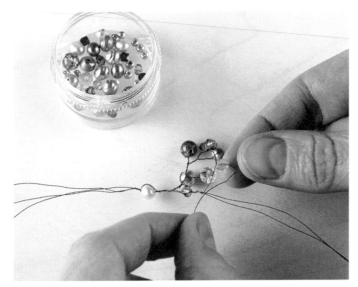

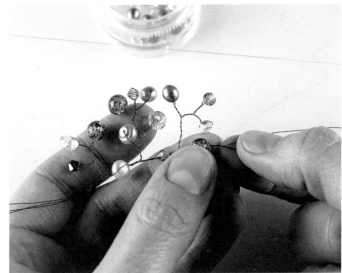

9 Thread a bead onto the wire. Hold the bead 5 mm (^{1}/$_4$ in) along the wire. Twist the wire on itself under the bead until you reach the rest of the short branch wire. Twist both wires together for 5 mm (^{1}/$_4$ in). Repeat to add another bead, then twist the wires together until you reach the other wires.

10 Repeat Steps 8 to 9 to make a short branch on the other side of the centre branch. Repeat Step 7 to 9 to make seven short branches each side of the centre branch. Use the longest wire for each branch so you do not run out of one wire.

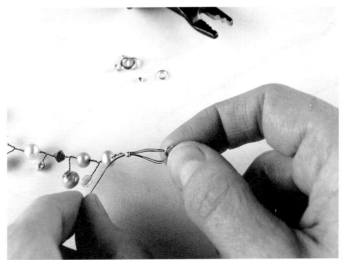

11 Repeat Step 7 on each side of the necklace. Thread a bead onto the longest wire. Hold the bead 5 mm (^{1}/$_4$ in) along the wire. Twist the wire on itself under the bead until you reach the other wires. Twist the three wires together for 3 mm (^{1}/$_8$ in). Repeat on each side of the necklace until the necklace is 40 cm (16 in) long.

12 Thread a crimp then a jump ring onto the three wires on one end of the necklace. Pull the wires back through the crimp. Adjust the crimp to sit 5 mm (^{1}/$_4$ in) after the last bead and the jump ring 5 mm (^{1}/$_4$ in) after the crimp. Secure the crimp with crimping pliers referring to the Fixing crimps technique on page 21. Snip off the excess wire. Repeat at the other end of the necklace. Fix the bolt ring clasp to the jump rings.

▼ Green twisted wire necklace

Here is a delicate choker with a 7-cm (2³/₄-in) long centre branch. The short branches are 5 cm (2 in) long. Pretty light green cube beads are threaded on the necklace and the wires twisted together between them.

▲ Purple twisted wire necklace

This elegant necklace of glass and plastic beads and pearls in shades of purple starts with a 110-cm (43-in) length of silver knitting wire. To make the first branch, thread a pearl onto the centre, twist the wires together three times to secure. Continue threading on beads and pearls onto one end of the wire for 8 cm (3¹/₄ in), twisting the wires together between the beads.

Thread a bead onto one end of the wire 8 cm (3¹/₄ in) from the first branch. Thread and secure beads as before until you reach the top of the first branch. Thread a bead onto the other wire 6.5 cm (2⁷/₈ in) from the first branch. Thread and secure beads as before until you reach the top of the first branch. Thread a 1-cm (³/₈-in) pearl onto one wire, twist both wires together three times on top of the pearl. Splay open the wires. Match the centre of the wires to the centre of an 80-cm (31¹/₂-in) length of wire. Twist the two wires together twice each side of the branches, thread beads and pearls onto one wire each side of the branches, twisting the wires together between the beads and pearls. Finish with crimps and a bolt ring clasp.

◄ Gold torque

This gold torque is bound with gold knitting wire with frosted plastic flower and butterfly shaped beads, white pearls and gold rocaille beads threaded on. The butterflies and rocaille beads are fixed following the Hanging beads technique on page 26.

To secure the trumpet shaped flowers, two 3-mm ($1/8$-in) white pearls are threaded onto the wire after the flower. One pearl is held 1.2 cm ($1/2$ in) above the flower, the wire is twisted on itself until it reaches the next pearl and is then threaded back through the flower. To finish, the wire is bound around the ends of the torque and stuck in place with superglue.

▶ Black wire pendant

Gauge 24 black wire is used to make three pendants on this necklace of black, silver, red and grey beads. A 40-cm (16-in) length of wire is used for the centre 6-cm ($2^1/2$-in) long branch. The two shorter branches are 4 cm ($1^1/2$ in) long. The wires are twisted together above the last bead on the branches and snipped 1 cm ($3/8$ in) above the last bead. The twisted wires are formed into a loop with a pair of round-nose pliers. The pendants hang from two 60-cm (24 in) lengths of black tiger tail. The centre branch is threaded onto the centre of one tiger tail. The other tiger tail is laid beside it and crimps are threaded onto both ends of the tiger tails and secured 2 cm ($3/4$ in) apart, enclosing the pendant. The shorter branches are threaded onto one tiger tail each side of the crimps and enclosed as before. Next, single beads are threaded onto one tiger tail and the tiger tails crimped together 2 cm ($3/4$ in) apart. The necklace is finished with crimps and a torpedo clasp.

Multi-strand choker

Three rows of pearls, clear beads and crystals are held in place with spacer bars on this pretty choker. The end bars have a loop at the back to attach to a jump ring and necklace clasp. The choker suspends delicate butterfly shaped crystals.

Materials and tools

1 silver screw necklace clasp

2 x 4-mm (^{5}/16-in) silver jump rings

2 silver three-hole end bars

4 silver three-hole spacer bars

4 butterfly shaped crystals

Approx. 18 x 4-mm (^{5}/16-in) bicone crystals

4 x 5.5-cm (2^1/4-in) silver head pins

Masking tape

135 cm (53 in) tiger tail

Approx. 65 x 4-mm (^{5}/16-in) cube shaped cream pearl beads

Approx. 80 assorted rock crystal chips and 4-mm (^{5}/16-in) clear beads

Approx. 55 pale pink potato shaped pearls

6 silver crimps

Tape measure

Wire cutters

Round-nose pliers

Snipe-nose pliers

1 Decide upon the finished length you wish the choker to be. Fix jump rings to the end bars, then to the necklace clasp. Measure the width of the end bars with the jump rings and clasp between them. Also measure the depth of the four three-hole bars. Take this measurement off the finished choker length. Divide the new measurement by five.

2 Thread one butterfly shaped crystal then a bicone crystal onto each head pin. Make a loop at the top following the Using head pins technique on page 24. Open the loop and slip it onto the bottom hole of each spacer bar. Close the loop with a pair of round- and snipe-nose pliers.

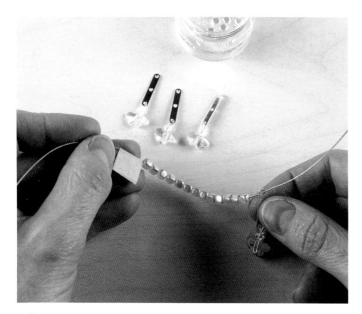

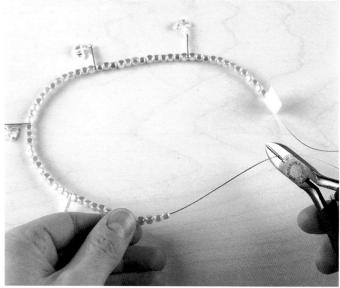

3 Snip three 45-cm (18-in) lengths of tiger tail. Wrap a piece of masking tape around each length about 7.5 cm (3 in) from one end to stop the beads slipping off. Thread on cube shaped cream pearl beads for the length of the final measurement on one tiger tail. Insert the tiger tail through the top hole of one bar.

4 Continue threading on beads until you have five equal sections of beads with bars between them. Snip off the tiger tail about 10 cm (4 in) from the last bead. Wrap the end of the tiger tail with masking tape.

5 On the second length of tiger tail, repeat to thread a mixture of rock crystal chips, 4-mm (5/16-in) clear beads and bicone crystals in the same way, but threading the tiger tail through the centre hole of the bars.

6 On the last length of tiger tail, repeat to thread on potato shaped pearls, threading the tiger tail through the lower hole of the bars.

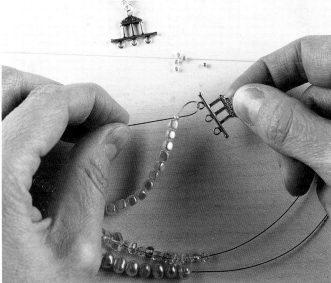

7 Check the length of the choker, allowing space for the end bars, jump rings and clasp. Remove the masking tape. Add beads at each end of the tiger tail to lengthen the choker or remove beads at each end to shorten it.

8 Thread a crimp onto one end of the top tiger tail. Thread the tiger tail through the top ring of one end bar. Pull the wire back through the crimp.

9 Adjust the crimp to sit close to the ring of the end bar. Secure the crimp with crimping pliers, referring to the Fixing crimps technique on page 21. Repeat on the second and third tiger tail to fix them to the second and third ring of the end bar.

10 Push the beads and bars along the tiger tails and fix to the other end bar with crimps as before.

◄ Green and turquoise choker

Here is a charming choker of two strands of 6-mm (^{1}/4-in) cylindrical beads. A contemporary silver charm hangs on two jump rings from each spacer bar. The lower strand of beads is longer at the centre and has a large glass heart pendant, a contemporary charm and an oval ring suspended at the centre on jump rings and a triangular pendant holder.

▶ Red and purple multi-strand necklace

This colourful necklace has five strands of beads. The beads are threaded on double lengths of Nymo thread. Each strand is tied to the rings of a five-hole end bar. Excess thread is threaded back through the beads and the knots dabbed with superglue. The first strand of alternate red bugle and rocaille beads is 51 cm (20 in) long and the following strands are each 2.5 cm (1 in) longer than the previous strand.

The second strand is of lilac rocaille beads; the third strand alternates pink metallic and glass rocaille beads; the fourth strand alternates 4-mm (^{5}/16-in) blue cube and lilac rocaille beads; and the fifth strand is worked in a sequence of a red 1-cm (^{3}/8-in) cylindrical bead, red rocaille bead, pink rocaille bead and another red rocaille bead.

◄ Antique pink multi-strand necklace

Unusual two-hole flat rectangular spacers are a main feature of this antique style necklace. The lower strand of dusky pink teardrop beads and gold rocaille beads are longer than the upper strand of gold beads so the necklace lays flat when worn.

▶ Red and lilac multi-strand necklace

This pretty necklace of three strands of vibrant glass beads are fixed to a three-hole box-and-tongue necklace clasp. The first strand of red and lilac rocaille beads is 44 cm (17$^{1}/_{4}$ in) long; the second strand of red 3-mm ($^{1}/_{8}$-in) diameter beads and rocaille beads is 45 cm (17$^{3}/_{4}$ in) long; and the third 46-cm (18$^{1}/_{4}$-in) strand of 6-mm ($^{1}/_{4}$-in) diameter red glass and lilac rocaille beads has a head pin threaded with a lilac glass heart bead and three assorted red beads at the centre.

Beader's tip

The measurements for this choker are worked out as follows:
- The finished length of the choker is 35 cm (13$^{3}/_{4}$ in).
- The width of the end bars with the jump rings and clasp between them is 5 cm (2 in).
- The depth of the four spacer bars together measures 5 mm ($^{1}/_{4}$ in).
- 35 cm (13$^{3}/_{4}$ in) minus 5 cm (2 in) and 5 mm ($^{1}/_{4}$ in) equals 29.5 cm (11$^{1}/_{2}$ in).

Pearl and cord lariat

Pearl and cord lariat

This elegant lariat is hung with crystal and pearl beads. The lariat is one metre (1 1/4 yd) long, the beads are fixed in groups of three to jump rings which are casually tied to a pale grey cord.

Materials and tools

Approx. 45 assorted crystal beads, ranging from 5 mm (1/4 in) to 1.2 cm (1/2 in) in diameter (two beads must be large enough to insert the cord through)

18 x 8-mm (5/32-in) white pearl beads

Approx. 30 size 7 clear silver lined rocaille beads

160 cm (1 3/4 yd) pale grey cord

54 x 5.5-cm (2 1/4-in) silver head pins

18 x 6-mm (1/4-in) silver jump rings
Superglue

Round-nose pliers
Wire cutters
Snipe-nose pliers
Embroidery scissors

1 Set aside two crystal beads that have holes large enough to insert the cord through. Thread 18 rocaille beads then 18 pearl beads onto head pins. Thread crystal beads onto the remaining head pins, placing larger beads singly and smaller beads in twos. If the holes of the crystal beads are large, thread a rocaille bead on first. Make a wrapped loop above the beads, referring to the Making wrapped loops technique on page 25.

2 Open the jump rings using two pairs of pliers. Slip two head pins with crystal beads and one head pin with a pearl bead onto each jump ring. Close the jump ring using the two pairs of pliers.

3 Thread one jump ring onto the cord. Tie the jump ring to the cord 15 cm (6 in) from one end. Continue tying the jump rings to the cord at 5 cm (2 in) intervals.

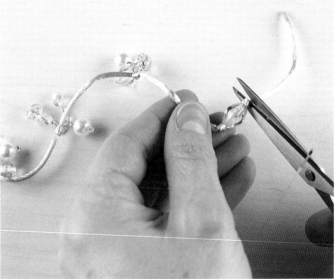

4 Knot the cord 5 cm (2 in) from the first and last knots. Thread one of the crystal beads set aside in Step 1 onto one end of the cord. Knot the cord under the bead.

5 Dab superglue on the extending cord close to the knot. Leave to dry, then cut the cord close to the knot. Repeat on the other end of the cord.

◀ Pink and apricot lariat

These sunshine colours will brighten the plainest summer outfit. The vibrant pink and apricot coloured pearls, plastic and miracle beads are hung on co-ordinating shaded embroidery thread. Amongst the beads on head pins with wrapped loops are plastic beads on triangular pendant holders. The beads are hung in groups of four, 6 cm (2¼ in) apart. The ends of the thread are finished with tag ends which suspend a jump ring of four beads.

Beader's tip

Apply all-purpose household glue to the end of the cord so it does not fray whilst you are working.

▲ Aquamarine shell necklace

If you prefer, finish the cord with a necklace fastening. This necklace has crystal drop beads fixed on pendant holders, dainty jade green shells fixed to jump rings, aquamarine pearl beads and jade green glass beads tied to fine silver cord. The ends of the cord are fixed to calottes between jump rings and a clasp and ring fastening.

◀◀ Chain lariat

A chain lariat hung with shiny beads is very effective and quick to achieve. Drilled hematite stones, grey cylindrical miracle beads, beige pearls and clear and black painted beads are hung on head pins with wrapped loops fixed on jump rings to a 70-cm (27½-in) silver chain at 3-cm (1¼-in) intervals.

◀ Vibrant lariat

This colourful gypsy style lariat has bright pink pearl beads, patterned black beads, multicoloured glittery beads and gold rocaille beads fixed on gold findings to an aquamarine cord.

Loop necklace

Loop necklace

This elegant necklace has a feature front fastening – one end of the necklace is simply slipped through a loop at the other end. Rock crystal chips and tiny round beads are highlighted by sapphire coloured crystals and a beautiful heart shaped pendant.

Materials and tools

Heart shaped sapphire pendant

Silver pendant holder with ring

18 x 6-mm ($^1/_4$-in) sapphire bicone crystals

76 rock crystal chips

10 x 6-mm ($^1/_4$-in) crystal star shaped beads

118 x 3-mm ($^1/_8$-in) rock crystal beads

White nylon twist thread

Superglue

Snipe-nose pliers

Round-nose pliers

Size 10 beading needle

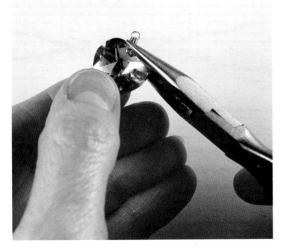

1 Slip the heart shaped sapphire pendant onto the pendant holder. Close the claws of the holder by squeezing them with a pair of snipe-nose pliers.

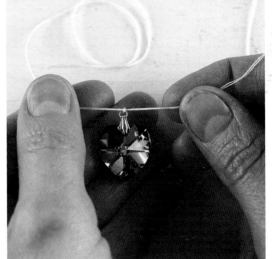

2 Thread a 110-cm (43-in) double length of thread on a beading needle. Slip the ring of the pendant holder onto the thread and tie it 25 cm (10 in) from the end of the thread. Leave the trailing end of thread.

3 Thread on one sapphire bicone crystal, 12 rock crystal chips, two star shaped beads and one sapphire bicone crystal.

4 Thread on 12 rock crystal round beads, one sapphire bicone crystal, eight rock crystal chips, one star shaped bead, then one sapphire bicone crystal.

5 Repeat Step 4 seven times. Thread on 22 rock crystal round beads for the loop.

6 Insert the needle back through the last sapphire crystal bead, the star and the rock crystal chips. Pull the thread to form the loop.

7 Part two chips close to the loop. Dab superglue on the thread to secure. Cut off the excess thread.

8 At the pendant end of the necklace, insert the needle back through the sapphire crystal bead and the rock crystal chips. Part two chips and dab superglue on the thread to secure. Cut off the excess thread.

▸ Hearts loop necklace

Stunning glass heart shaped beads are a lovely feature on this richly coloured necklace. One blue rocaille bead and three 1.5-cm (5/8-in) striped hearts are at one end of the necklace, then 5-mm (1/4-in) green metallic beads, blue rocaille beads and 1.5-cm (5/8-in) and 1-cm (3/8-in) heart shaped beads are threaded along its length with a loop of blue rocaille and green metallic beads.

▾ Leaf loop necklace

Here is a delicately coloured necklace of rectangular beads in shades of pink, ochre and green. A lovely leaf shaped pendant is hung on a triangular pendant holder followed by three 8-mm (5/32-in) pink metal beads. The necklace is then worked in a sequence of five rectangular beads and one pink metallic bead. There are two pale pink rocaille beads between each larger bead. Eight rectangular beads form the loop.

Beader's tip

Make sure the loop is large enough for the beads at the other end of the necklace to slip through. Increase the number of beads in the loop if necessary before finishing the necklace.

▴ Brown loop necklace

Single brown triangular glass beads are threaded between a sequence of 12 copper rocaille beads. Twenty-seven rocaille beads form the loop and the other end has three triangular beads with a single rocaille bead between them.

▾ Turquoise cube loop necklace

This long loop necklace has a sequence of a turquoise fibre optic cube bead, a bronze bugle bead, a grey rocaille bead and another bugle bead. The loop is formed with alternating bugle beads and five rocaille beads. A 1-cm (3/8-in) diameter bronze bead, fibre optic bead and a rocaille bead are at the other end.

Silk flower choker

Silk flower choker

There is a beautiful selection of silk flowers available nowadays and they can be taken apart to use to make jewellery. This elegant choker of velvet ribbon has a bold red flower highlighted with beads and uses various bead embroidery techniques.

Materials and tools

40 cm (16 in) 2-cm (³/4-in) wide red edged blue velvet ribbon

Blue and red sewing thread

25 g (1 oz) size 9 blue rocaille beads

1.2-cm (¹/2-in) red button with two holes

Red silk flower with two sets of petals

25 g (1 oz) size 9 red rocaille beads

28 x 1.2-cm (¹/2-in) blue bugle beads

9 x 5-mm (¹/4-in) pale blue bicone crystals

Embroidery scissors

Size 10 bead embroidery needle

Dressmaking pin

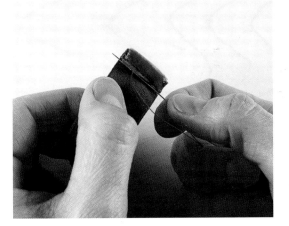

1 Cut a length of ribbon long enough to wrap comfortably around your neck plus 3 cm (1¹/4 in). Turn under 5 mm (¹/4 in) twice at each end and sew in place to hem the ends of the choker.

2 Thread a needle with a double length of blue thread. Bring the needle through one end of the choker 5 mm (¹/4 in) above the lower edge. Thread on enough blue rocaille beads to loop around the button. Fasten the thread 5 mm (¹/4 in) below the upper edge. Repeat to attach the loop securely.

3 Try on the choker again and carefully mark the position of the button under the loop with a pin. Bring the needle threaded with a double length of thread to the right side at the pinned mark. Thread on two blue rocaille beads and insert the needle up through one of the button holes.

4 Thread on three blue rocaille beads and insert the needle back through the other hole and the first two beads. Pull the thread so the button sits on the first two beads. Repeat to secure the button.

5 To create the picot beaded edge on the ribbon. Bring a needle threaded with a single length of red thread up through the edge of the ribbon at one end. Thread on three red rocaille beads. Insert the needle into the edge of the ribbon 3 mm ($^1/_8$ in) from where it emerged and bring it out 1.2 cm ($^1/_2$ in) further on and continue along both edges of the ribbon.

6 Take the flower apart and discard the plastic parts that hold the petals together. To edge the petals with beads, bring a needle threaded with a single length of thread to the right side 3 mm ($^1/_8$ in) inside the outer edge. Thread on four red rocaille beads. Lay the beads along the petal 3 mm ($^1/_8$ in) inside the outer edge. Insert the needle after the last bead.

7 Bring the needle to the right side between the second and third bead. Insert the needle through the third and fourth bead. Thread on four beads as before and continue outlining the petals. Lay one set of petals on top of the other, alternating the petals. Try the choker on and pin the flower in position.

8 Bring a needle threaded with a single length of blue thread to the right side through the centre of the flower. To make a stamen, thread on one blue bugle bead and one blue rocaille bead. Insert the needle back through the bugle bead and pull the thread so the bugle bead stands upright. Add five more stamens around the first.

9 Sew five pale blue bicone crystals around the stamens. Catch the flower petals to the choker with a few small stitches so the top petals do not flop over with the weight of the beads.

10 Refer to the Hanging beads technique on page 26 to make four lengths of hanging beads suspended from the ribbon below the flower. Make the hanging beads 9.5 cm (3 3/4 in), 8 cm (3 1/4 in), 6.5 cm (2 1/2 in), and 5 cm (2 in) long with a sequence of one bugle bead, one blue rocaille bead, one pale blue bicone crystal and one blue rocaille bead at the ends.

▶ Cream flower necklace

Here is a pretty necklace of creamy silk flower heads dotted along a 50-cm (20-in) gold cord. The flower heads are applied 3 cm (1 1/4 in) apart with a single rocaille bead at the centre. A mother-of-pearl sequin is sewn at the back of the cord under the flower with a single bead. A strand of gold rocaille beads is twisted around the cord between the flowers, and the cord ends are finished with tag ends and fastened with a diamante box-and-tongue clasp.

◀ Pink rose necklace

A vibrant pink flower is sewn to the centre of a length of matching satin ribbon. Square crystals are sewn to the centre of the flower and surrounded by loops of rocaille beads. Four lengths of hanging beads with square crystals at the ends hang below the flower.

To edge the ribbon, thread on 10 size 11 rocaille beads on the right side of the ribbon. Insert the needle through the wrong side of the ribbon 1.2 cm (1/2 in) from where you started, continue along both edges of the ribbon. The necklace is finished by hemming the raw ends and slipping an 8-mm (5/16-in) jump ring through the hem, which is fixed to a smaller jump ring and box-and-tongue necklace clasp.

▶ Lilac fringed choker

This delicate lilac choker features a row of 17 tiny silk flower heads sewn along the centre of an 80-cm (31$^1/_2$-in) organza ribbon. Each flower head is secured with a lilac rocaille bead. A fringe of rocaille beads hangs below the flowers. The longest length of 6 cm (2$^1/_4$ in) hangs below the centre flower. The fringe then graduates to the shortest lengths of 2 cm ($^3/_4$ in) below the outer flowers. Three lengths of hanging beads hang at each end of the ribbon with a flower head on each side of the ribbon.

◀ Black rose choker

A ready-made beaded band is used to make this stylish black and silver choker. A loop of silver rocaille beads and an antique button fasten the ends. A black silk rose sewn to the choker is dotted with silver rocaille beads. Silver rocaille beads with clear bicone crystals at the ends hang below the rose amongst loops of beads.

Beader's tip

If the button has a shank, simply sew it on without using beads as the shank will allow the button to stand proud of the choker and so fasten neatly.

Spiral link necklace

Spiral link necklace

Hung with crystal beads and dainty hearts, this necklace would make a lovely bridal gift. The stylised S-shaped links are hand crafted with wire and a pair of round-nose pliers.

Materials and tools

50 cm (20 in) gauge 20 silver wire

Chinagraph pencil

Masking tape

7 x 1-cm ($^3/_8$-in) crystal heart beads

7 x 2.5-cm (1-in) silver head pins

16 x 6-mm ($^1/_4$-in) oval crystal beads

26 silver eye pins

2 x 4-mm ($^5/_{32}$-in) silver jump rings

1 silver clasp-and-ring necklace fastening

Wire cutters

Round-nose pliers

Snipe-nose pliers

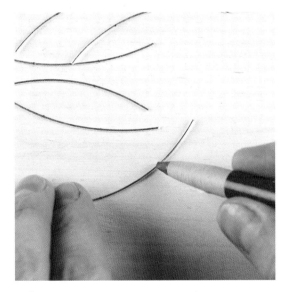

1 Snip seven 6-cm (2$^1/_4$-in) lengths of gauge 20 silver wire for the links. Divide the wires into three 2-cm ($^3/_4$-in) sections by marking them with a Chinagraph pencil.

2 Stick a 5-mm ($^1/_4$-in) wide strip of masking tape around one jaw of a pair of round-nose pliers 8 mm ($^5/_{16}$ in) from the tips; this will help keep the links the same size.

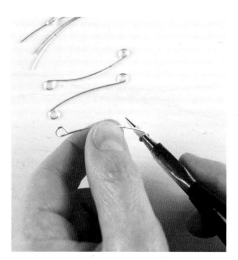

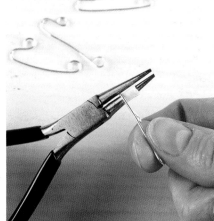

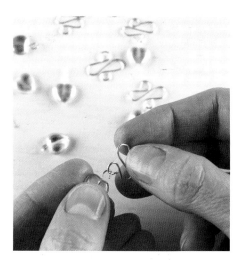

3 Hold one end of a wire with the pliers at the inner edge of the tape. Bend the wire around the jaw until it meets the wire again, forming a ring. Repeat at the other end of the wire but turning the wire in the opposite direction.

4 Hold the wire with the pliers at one pencil mark level with the inner edge of the tape. Bend the wire downwards in a U shape. Repeat at the other end of the wire but bending the wire in the opposite direction. Repeat to make seven wire links. Gently squeeze the links between your fingers to make a figure of eight shape.

5 Slip the crystal hearts onto head pins. Snip the wire 8 mm ($^5/_{16}$ in) above the beads. Refer to the Using head pins technique on page 24 to make a loop above the bead. Slightly open the loop on the head pins and slip it onto the lower circle of each link. Close the loops.

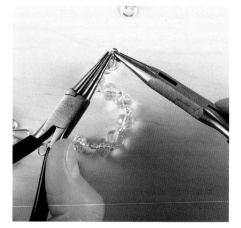

6 Slip each oval crystal bead onto an eye pin. Make a loop above the bead, referring to the Making pinned beads technique on page 24.

7 Slightly open the loops on the pinned beads. Slip each side of a link onto the open loops to fix a pinned bead between each link. Close the loops. Join two lengths of ten pinned beads together and fix each length to the end links. Close the loops.

8 Fix a jump ring to the pinned beads at each end of the necklace. Fix a necklace fastening to the jump rings.

▲ Coloured hearts link necklace

This delicate necklace has nine links suspending coloured glass hearts. The links are joined with pinned beads of two green glass beads. Silver chains are fixed to the last pinned beads and the necklace fastens with a lobster claw fastening.

Beader's tip

File the ends of the shaped wire links with a metal file to remove any sharp edges. A metal emery nail file is ideal.

▲ Frosted pendant

This frosted glass heart pendant hangs on a pendant holder from a pinned cream oval pearl which hangs from a jump ring. Two elegant silver links are formed from 6-cm ($2^1/_4$-in) lengths of 24-gauge silver wire.

The wire is bent in a U shape 2 cm ($^3/_4$ in) from one end with a pair of round-nose pliers. A circle is formed at each end by bending the wire around one spoke of the pliers. The longer leg of the wire is then formed by hand in a gentle curve. A jump ring is fixed between the jump ring on the pinned bead and the U of each link. Single frosted plastic beads and rows of three cream oval pearls are pinned at each end.

▼ Blue wire necklace

Vibrant blue wire is a stunning feature of this linked necklace. Eight 6-cm ($2^1/_4$-in) lengths of gauge 20 wire are formed into stylised Ws by bending them in half with round-nose pliers. The wire is then bent upwards 2 cm ($^3/_4$ in) from each end, again with round-nose pliers. The ends are then bent around one jaw of the pliers to form a circle at each end. A 1.5-cm ($^5/_8$-in) long red or pink plastic disc bead is pinned on gauge 24 blue wire between each link.

Four pinned red bugle beads are fixed to the last links and finish with a jump ring. The pinned beads and jump rings are handmade from wire (see the Pinning beads and Making jump rings technique on page 23). Narrow ribbon is sewn to the jump rings for fastening.

▼ Red and gold link necklace

Gold wire is used to make five links on this regal necklace. Red glass spear shaped pendants hang on two jump rings from each link. The links are joined with four pinned red beads each side of the links. Five gold space beads embossed with a spiral design are fixed between jump rings to the last pinned beads. A screw necklace fastening fastens the necklace.

Charm necklace

Charm necklace

Making a charm necklace is a great way to use odd beads and charms. Gather together an interesting mix of glass, plastic and metal pieces to suspend from a chain.

Materials and tools

Approx. 34 glass, plastic and metal pendants, charms and beads

Approx. 34 pendant holders

Approx. 34 x 5.5-cm (2^1/$_4$-in) silver head pins

Approx. 104 x 4-mm (^{5}/$_{32}$-in) silver jump rings

46 cm (18 in) silver chain

1 screw necklace clasp

Snipe-nose pliers
Round-nose pliers
Wire cutters

1 Prepare the pendants and charms by hanging them on pendant holders or jump rings. See the Using jump rings and Fixing a pendant holder techniques on pages 21 and 26 respectively. Fix beads onto head pins following the Using head pins technique on page 24.

2 Fix a jump ring to all the pendant holders and jump rings of the pendants, charms and loops of the head pins. Arrange all the pendants, charms and beads in a row in a pleasing mix of shapes and colours. Very small charms can be hung on a jump ring with a larger pendant behind.

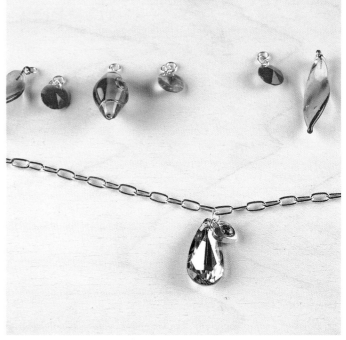

3 Check which direction the pendant or charm will hang in when hung on the chain. If the pendants and charms are flat and need to face forward, fix another jump ring to the last one.

4 Starting at the centre of the chain, slip the top jump ring of one item to one link. Close the jump ring securely.

5 Continue fixing the top jump rings of all the pieces to each chain link, working outwards from the centre.

6 Fix a jump ring to each end of the chain. Fix a screw necklace clasp to the jump rings.

▲ Gold charm necklace

Here, a necklace of ochre coloured chips threaded on Nymo thread has five antique looking gold charms on jump rings threaded on 2.5 cm (1 in) apart at the front of the necklace. The necklace is finished with calottes, jump rings and a pretty vintage style clasp.

▼ Aquamarine pendant

This pretty necklace has a jump ring fixed to the centre. A 4-cm (1 1/2-in) length of chain hangs from the jump ring. Aquamarine chips and pearls, clear and aquamarine crystals and glass beads on head pins and clear glass drop beads on triangular pendant holders are fixed to the chain links 8 mm (^{5}/$_{32}$ in) apart at the front of the necklace. Five 4-mm (^{5}/$_{16}$-in) aquamarine crystals are pinned between the chain links each side of the hanging beads 1.5 cm (^{5}/$_8$ in) apart.

▲ Pink and ochre charm necklace

This 60-cm (24-in) gold chain has 34 1.5-cm (^{5}/$_8$-in) plastic discs in co-ordinating shades of pink, lilac and ochre. The discs are attached with triangular pendant holders to every other link at the front of the chain.

▼ Turquoise charm necklace

Bright turquoise glass and pearlised beads are fixed on head pins on this bold chain necklace. Any beads with large holes have a small gold bead at the bottom of the head pin and a small turquoise and a gold bead on top to stop the large bead slipping off. The beads are hung with a gold shell shaped charm in nine groups of three on 8-mm (^{5}/$_{32}$-in) jump rings which are fixed to the front of the chain 2.5 cm (1 in) apart.

Two star shaped charms are fixed to each end of a 7.5-cm (3-in) length of fine chain with 3-mm (^{1}/$_8$-in) jump rings. A 3-mm (^{1}/$_8$-in) jump ring is fixed 2.5 cm (1 in) from one end of the fine chain and fixed to one of the large jump rings on the chain.

Beader's tip

When making the necklace, keep checking that all the jump rings suspending the pendants, charms and beads hang from the bottom of the chain links.

Daisy choker

Daisy choker

This lovely choker uses a distinctive daisy beading technique. Any size round bead is suitable to make the daisy but the beads must all be the same size.

Materials and tools

Approx. 131 size 9 clear rocaille beads
66 size 9 silver rocaille beads
11 size 9 gold rocaille beads
White Nymo thread
2 x 6-mm (^{1}/4-in) silver jump rings
Superglue
50 cm (20 in) of 5-mm (^{1}/4-in) wide gold
  ribbon

Size 10 beading needle
Single bead to use as a stop bead
Snipe-nose pliers
Round-nose pliers
Dress-making pin

1 Thread a beading needle with a double 120-cm (47-in) length of thread. Attach a stop bead to the end of the thread, leaving a 25-cm (10-in) trailing end of thread. Thread on 60 clear beads.

2 To form one daisy, thread on four silver beads: these will be the 'petals'.

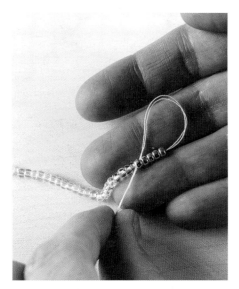

3 Thread on one gold bead. Insert the needle back through the first silver bead towards the stop bead.

4 Thread on two silver beads and take the needle through the fourth silver bead in the opposite direction. Pull the thread so the silver beads form a circle around the gold bead.

5 Thread on one clear bead. Repeat Steps 2 to 4 to make a row of 11 daisies with a clear bead between each daisy. Thread on 60 clear beads.

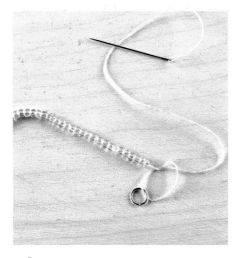

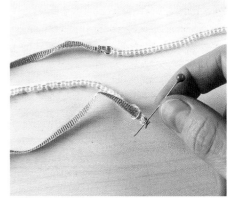

6 Remove the stop bead. Thread on a jump ring and tie it to the thread with a double knot.

7 Insert the needle back through the last fifteen beads. Pull the thread and cut off the excess thread close to the beads. Dot the knot with superglue to secure it. Fix a jump ring to the other end of the choker in the same way.

8 Cut the ribbon in half. Slip one end of one ribbon through one jump ring. Pin under 5 mm ($1/4$ in) on the ribbon. Fold the pinned end over the jump ring and sew it neatly to the ribbon with gold sewing thread. Attach the other ribbon to the other jump ring. Cut the extending ends of ribbon diagonally.

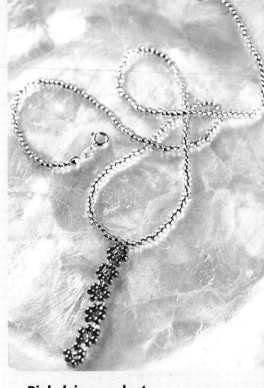

▲ Blue daisy necklace

Adapt the daisy technique so that the daisies hang from a necklace of rocaille beads. Thread on a sequence of six size 11 turquoise rocaille beads and three size 7 pale blue glass rocaille beads eight times. Thread on two size 7 pale blue glass rocaille beads. Thread on four 5-mm ($1/4$-in) jade green glass beads then one 5-mm ($1/4$-in) pale blue glass bead. Insert the needle back through the first jade green bead towards the start of the necklace.

Thread on two 5-mm ($1/4$-in) jade green glass beads and take the needle through the fourth, third, second and first jade green bead. Pull the thread so the jade green beads form a circle around the pale blue bead. Insert the needle through the last size 7 pale blue glass rocaille bead to continue the necklace. Thread on one size 7 pale blue glass rocaille bead. Thread on a sequence of six size 11 turquoise rocaille beads, three size 7 pale blue glass rocaille beads, six size 11 turquoise rocaille beads and two size 7 pale blue glass rocaille beads and a daisy six times. Thread on rocaille beads to match the other end of the necklace and finish with calottes and a lobster claw clasp.

▲ Yellow and green daisy necklace

The daisy technique is used here to make a long necklace of pastel yellow and green beads. There are five yellow beads between each daisy. This necklace is 120 cm (47 in) long and fastens with a lobster claw fastening.

Beader's tip

If necessary, adjust the length of the choker after Step 5. To do this, remove the stop bead, then remove the same number of beads from each end to shorten the choker or thread the same number of beads onto each end to lengthen it.

▶ Flower bead necklace

Here is a cheat's version of the daisy technique. Pretty flower shaped beads have been threaded between a sequence of 14 rocaille beads to make this necklace. The necklace is finished with calottes and a bolt ring fastening.

▲ Pink daisy pendant

This pretty pendant is made by threading pale pink glass rocaille beads onto thread for 22 cm ($8 1/2$ in). Another pale pink glass rocaille bead is threaded on, then six daisies with pink metallic rocaille bead petals and a single pale pink glass rocaille bead are worked along the thread to form the pendant. The needle is threaded back through the daisies to reach the necklace. The needle is then threaded back through the last pale pink bead. Pale pink beads are threaded on for 22 cm ($8 1/2$ in) to make the other half of the necklace. Calottes and a bolt ring fastening complete the necklace.

Organza pendant

Organza pendant

This handsome pendant has a cascade of glass drop beads hanging from fine organza ribbons. The beads are fixed to a short chain of jump rings so they hang at different levels.

Materials and tools

13 x 2.5-cm (1-in) light blue frosted glass drop beads

13 x 5.5-cm ($2^1/4$-in) silver head pins

2 x 1.5-cm ($5/8$-in) light blue sparkling glass drop beads

2 x 6-mm ($1/4$-in) light blue sparkling round beads

2 x 5.5-cm ($2^1/4$-in) silver eye pins

10 x 8-mm ($5/16$-in) silver jump rings

140 cm ($1^1/2$ yd) of 5-mm ($1/4$-in) wide pink organza ribbon

2 silver calottes

Superglue

2 x 4-mm ($5/32$-in) silver jump rings

Silver clasp and ring necklace fastening

Wire cutters

Round-nose pliers

Snipe-nose pliers

12 cm (5 in) of knitting wire

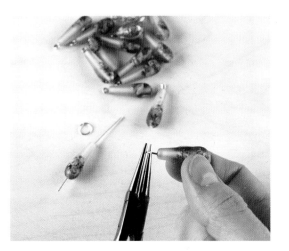

1 Fix the drop beads on head pins following the Using head pins technique on page 24. Slip the loop on the head pin of one of the frosted drop beads onto an 8-mm ($5/16$-in) jump ring. Close the ring with two pairs of pliers. This drop bead will be at the bottom of the pendant.

2 Slip another jump ring onto the first jump ring. Hang one frosted drop bead each side of the first jump ring, then close the ring.

3 Add four more jump rings with two frosted drop beads threaded on and the last jump ring positioned between them to start to form the pendant. Add the seventh jump ring with two sparkling drop beads threaded on and the last jump ring positioned between them. Add the eighth jump ring with two frosted drop beads threaded on and the last jump ring positioned between them. The pendant is now complete.

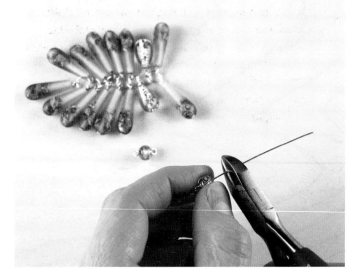

4 Fix each sparkling round bead on an eye pin following the Making pinned beads technique on page 24. Open the top jump ring and slip a pinned bead on each side. Close the jump ring.

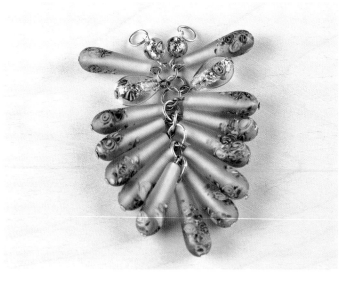

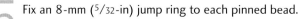

5 Fix an 8-mm (^{5}/32-in) jump ring to each pinned bead.

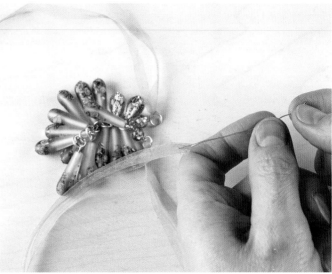

6 Cut two 68-cm (27-in) lengths of organza ribbon. Fold one ribbon in half. Slip the loop of the ribbon through the jump ring of one pinned bead. Pull the ends of the ribbon through the loop. Repeat on the other pinned bead. Pull the ribbons tight to suspend the pendant. Lay the ribbons flat one on top of the other each side of the pendant.

7 Insert a 12-cm (5-in) length of 0.24 knitting wire through the ends of the ribbon. Fold the wire in half to make a wire needle. Twist the ends of the wire together twice.

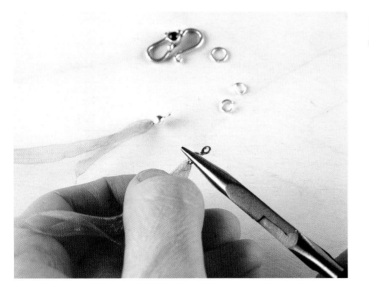

8 Thread the wire needle through the hole in a calotte. Cut off the needle and tie the ribbon in a knot. Dab superglue in one cup of the calotte. Close the cups with a pair of flat-nose pliers enclosing the ribbon knot. Repeat on the end of the other ribbon. Fix a 4-mm (5/32-in) jump ring to each calotte. Finally, fix a necklace fastening to the jump rings.

▶ Organza and pearl pendant

Here, nine pretty freshwater pearls are threaded onto a black head pin and fixed to a jump ring. Twelve single pearls are threaded on head pins and fixed in groups of three to jump rings. The jump rings are slipped onto the first jump ring: two each side of the long beaded head pin. The jump ring is tied to a length of organza ribbon. The ends of the ribbon are painted with clear nail varnish before cutting to prevent them fraying.

◀ Crystal spears pendant

A delicate pendant of crystal spears fixed to triangular pendant holders hangs from a necklace of clear glass beads.

Beader's tip

For a similar effect, beads on head pins can be fixed to the links of a short length of chain to hang from a ribbon.

▸ Grey organza pendant

A beautiful quartz drop bead fixed on a triangular pendant holder is tied to the centre of a grey organza ribbon on this charming pendant necklace. Four 8-mm ($5/16$-in) lilac drop beads are fixed to jump rings and tied to the ribbon 3 cm ($1^{1}/4$ in) apart at each side of the pendant. The ribbon ends are fixed in calottes between jump rings and a lobster clasp fastening.

▸ Ochre spears pendant

This pendant of nine ochre coloured spears fixed to triangular pendant holders has a bronze bead pinned at each side onto a fine gold chain.

Knotted amethyst necklace

Knotted amethyst necklace

The simple technique of securing beads to a cord by tying them onto the cord with bead string gives a lovely chunky, tactile effect especially if the beads are of different shapes and sizes.

Materials and tools

Purple size 8 nylon bead string

Assorted amethyst and purple glass, plastic and pearl beads, ranging from 5 mm (^{1}/$_4$ in) to 1.5 cm (^{5}/$_8$ in) in diameter

45 cm (18 in) purple cord

Superglue

2 gold tag ends

2 x 6-mm (^{1}/$_4$-in) gold jump rings

1 gold clasp and ring necklace fastening

Size 7 embroidery needle

Embroidery scissors

Snipe-nose pliers

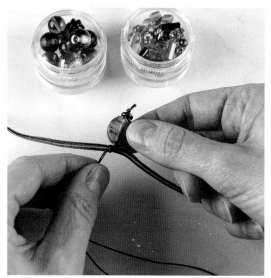

1 Thread a needle with a double length of bead string and knot the ends together. Thread on a large bead. If the hole is too large for the knot, thread on a smaller bead first.

2 Tie the threads around the centre of the cord with a single overhand knot close to the bead.

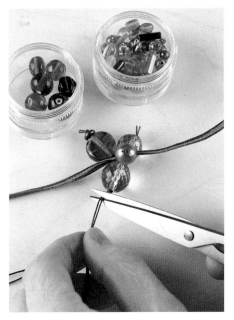

3 Thread on another large bead. Knot the threads on top of the bead. Trim the thread ends 5 mm (¹/₄ in) above the knots.

4 Tie another two beads to the cord in the same way, close to the first two beads.

5 Working outwards from the centre, continue tying beads to the cord, starting with the largest and graduating to the smallest. Push the beads close together as you work so the cord is not visible. Tie on beads to cover 20 cm (8 in) at the centre of the cord.

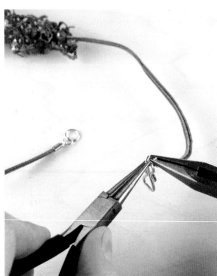

6 Glue each end of the cord onto a tag end. Fold over the sides of the tag ends with a pair of snipe-nose pliers, referring to the Fixing a tag end technique on page 27.

7 Open the jump rings and slip each ring onto the loop of one tag end. Fix the necklace clasp fastening onto the jump rings.

Beader's tip

To keep the shape of the necklace symmetrical, work outwards from the centre, building up both sides of the necklace at the same time.

▶ Knotted green and blue necklace

Thirty green 5-mm (^{1}/4-in) cube beads, an 8-mm (^{5}/16-in) blue bead, six 2-cm (^{3}/4-in) heart shaped beads, an 8-mm (^{5}/16-in) blue bead and 30 khaki green 5-mm (^{1}/4-in) cube beads are threaded onto Nymo thread. A mixture of 16 green cube and 8-mm (^{5}/16-in) blue beads are tied to the thread with green bead string between the heart beads. The necklace is finished with calottes and a lobster claw fastening.

▲ Knotted turquoise necklace

Turquoise glass and plastic beads are tied to the centre of a 60-cm (24-in) length of turquoise cord for 10 cm (4 in). Larger beads are concentrated at the centre of the necklace.

▲ Knotted brown necklace

This tying technique works well with smaller beads too. Here, 4–6-mm (^{5}/32–^{1}/4-in) diameter brown and silver beads are tied with brown bead string to a beige thong.

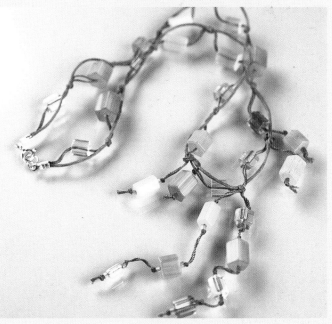

▲ Knotted pastel necklace

This casual necklace has clear and pastel coloured glass cylindrical beads threaded onto lilac bead strings, tied to a fine lilac cotton cord. Two 75-cm (29^1/2-in) lengths of bead string and one of cord are tied together at the centre, catching in the centre of a 30-cm (12-in) double length of bead string.

A cylindrical bead is threaded onto the double strings each side of the centre and the strings and cord knotted together 3 cm (1^1/4 in) from the centre knot, catching in the centre of a 20-cm (8-in) double length of bead string. Cylindrical beads and a lilac rocaille bead are threaded and the ends knotted under the last beads. Shorter hanging strings are added each side of the centre and the excess strings cut off below the knots.

The necklace is continued by knotting the strings and cord together 3 cm (1^1/4 in) apart with a single cylindrical bead threaded onto the double strings between each knot. The necklace is finished with tag ends and a bolt ring fastening.

Vintage necklace

This regal necklace may look complicated but is easy to construct using three lengths of thread: one for the necklace, one for the outer loops and one for the centre loop.

Materials and tools

Purple Nymo thread

25 g (1 oz) size 9 dark pink rocaille beads

12 x 6-mm (^{1}/4-in) dark pink bicone crystals

10 x 8-mm (^{5}/16-in) dark pink bicone crystals

7 x 1-cm (^{3}/8-in) purple teardrop crystals

10 x 6-mm (^{1}/4-in) purple bicone crystals

2 x 3-mm (^{1}/8-in) purple bicone crystals

1 x 1.5-cm (^{5}/8-in) pink crystal pendant

1 silver pendant holder with ring

3 x 4-mm (^{5}/32-in) silver jump rings

2 silver calottes

Silver box-and-tongue necklace clasp

3 size 10 beading needles

5 beads to use as stop beads

Round-nose pliers

Snipe-nose pliers

Superglue

1 Thread one beading needle with a 90-cm (1-yd) double length of Nymo thread. Anchor a stop bead 20 cm (8 in) from the end of the thread (see the Stop bead technique on page 22). Thread on 70 dark pink rocaille beads.

2 Thread on one 6-mm (^{1}/4-in) dark pink bicone crystal, nine rocaille beads, one 6-mm (^{1}/4-in) dark pink bicone crystal, nine rocaille beads and another 6-mm (^{1}/4-in) dark pink bicone crystal.

3 Now thread on 13 rocaille beads, one 8-mm ($5/16$-in) dark pink bicone crystal, one purple teardrop crystal, one 8-mm ($5/16$-in) dark pink bicone crystal then five rocaille beads.

4 Thread on two 6-mm ($1/4$-in) purple bicone crystals, two 6-mm ($1/4$-in) dark pink bicone crystals. Thread on one purple teardrop crystal which will be the centre of the necklace.

5 Continue threading on beads and crystals to symmetrically match the first half of the necklace. Fix a stop bead after the last bead to stop the beads slipping off.

6 Thread the remaining beading needles with a 110-cm (43-in) double length of Nymo thread. Anchor a stop bead 20 cm (8 in) from the end of the threads. Insert one needle and thread through the necklace and bring it out after the third 6-mm ($1/4$-in) dark pink bicone crystal. To make the first outer loop, thread on 22 rocaille beads, one 6-mm ($1/4$-in) purple bicone crystal, one 8-mm ($5/16$-in) dark pink bicone crystal, one purple teardrop crystal, one 8-mm ($5/16$-in) dark pink bicone crystal and one 6-mm ($1/4$-in) purple bicone crystal. Now thread on eight rocaille beads.

7 On the necklace, insert the needle and thread through the nine crystals at the centre. Bring the needle out after the last crystal.

8 Thread on beads to symmetrically match the first outer loop. Insert the needle through the necklace starting at the eighth 6-mm (¹/₄-in) dark pink bicone crystal and continue to the end of the necklace. Fix a stop bead after the last bead.

9 Fix a pendant holder to the pendant, squeezing the jaws closed with a pair of snipe-nose pliers. Slip a jump ring through the hole of the pendant holder, close the jump ring with the pliers.

10 Insert the remaining needle and thread through the necklace and bring it out before the first 6-mm (¹/₄-in) purple bicone crystal. To start the centre loop, insert the needle down through the last three rocaille beads of the outer loop.

11 Thread on seven rocaille beads, one 6-mm (¹/₄-in) purple bicone crystal, one 6-mm (¹/₄-in) dark pink bicone crystal, one 8-mm (⁵/₁₆-in) dark pink bicone crystal, one purple teardrop crystal, one 3-mm (¹/₈in) purple bicone crystal, the jump ring on the pendant holder, one 3-mm (¹/₈-in) purple bicone crystal, one purple teardrop crystal, one 8-mm (⁵/₁₆-in) dark pink bicone crystal, one 6-mm (¹/₄-in) dark pink bicone crystal and one 6-mm (¹/₄-in) purple bicone crystal. Thread on seven rocaille beads.

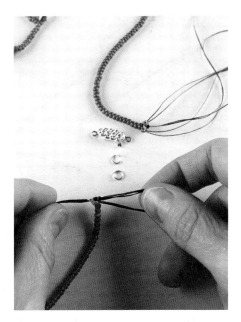

12 Insert the needle up through the last three beads of the outer loop. Continue to the end of the necklace.

13 Remove the stop beads. Refer to the Fixing calottes and Fixing a necklace clasp techniques on pages 27 and 22 respectively.

◂ Lilac and amethyst vintage necklace

This pretty necklace of lilac rocaille beads and amethyst chips is created with three lengths of thread, one for the necklace, one for the shallow loops and one for the centre loop.

Beader's tip

Before you start, make sure the holes in the crystals and beads are large enough to take three double lengths of thread.

▸ Grey and jet vintage necklace

To make this dainty grey and jet necklace, thread on 78 size 9 grey rocaille beads. Next, thread on a sequence of one 4-mm ($^5/_{32}$-in) jet bicone bead and 14 grey rocaille beads three times. Thread on another jet bead. Thread on one rocaille bead to mark the centre of the necklace.

Thread the other half of the necklace symmetrically. Insert a second length of thread through the necklace, bringing the needle out before the first jet bead. Thread on 18 grey rocaille beads, one jet spear and 13 grey rocaille beads. Insert the needle through the second jet bead towards the start of the necklace to form a loop. Repeat to make two more loops, bringing the needle out after the centre rocaille bead.

Make a length of 58 hanging rocaille beads with a jet spear at the end. Insert the needle through the centre bead towards the end of the necklace and make three symmetrical loops. The necklace is finished with black calottes, jump rings and a lobster claw fastening.

▲ Pendant vintage necklace

Here is a sparkling necklace of pearls, metallic rocaille beads, pale green ceramic beads and crystals that would make a beautiful gift for a bride. There are two lengths of thread, one for the necklace and the other for the centre loop with a crystal teardrop pendant at the centre.

▲ Fringed vintage necklace

This shimmering fringed necklace is made with two lengths of thread, one for the necklace and the other for the fringes. The necklace is threaded on an 80-cm ($31^1/_2$-in) double length of thread with silver rocaille beads interspersed with 6-mm ($^1/_4$-in) diameter iridescent beads. A fringe of nine lengths of hanging beads is worked at the front of the necklace, graduating in size from the centre.

Long crystal necklace

Long crystal necklace

This 155-cm (61-in) long shimmering necklace is very versatile. It can be worn single, double, in thirds or bound around the neck as a dramatic choker. Choose a mixture of pretty co-ordinating colours to work with.

Materials and tools

180 cm (2 yd) Nymo thread

200 x size 9 lilac rocaille beads

40 x 4-mm (^{5}/32-in) pale pink plastic beads

80 x 3-mm (^{1}/8-in) bright pink crystal beads

40 x 4-mm (^{5}/32-in) clear glass beads

120 x size 9 pale pink rocaille beads

40 x 4-mm (^{5}/32-in) bright pink plastic beads

19 x 8-mm (^{5}/16-in) purple glass beads

2 x 5-mm (^{1}/4-in) silver jump rings

2 calottes

Silver torpedo necklace clasp

Superglue

Size 10 beading needle

1 bead to use as a stop bead

Round-nose pliers

Snipe-nose pliers

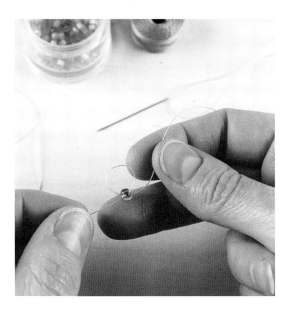

1 Thread a 90 cm (1 yd) double length of Nymo thread on the beading needle. Anchor the stop bead 25 cm (10 in) from the end of the thread (see the Stop bead technique on page 22).

2 Thread on one lilac rocaille bead, one pale pink plastic bead, one lilac rocaille bead, one bright pink crystal, one lilac rocaille bead, one clear glass bead, two lilac rocaille beads, one bright pink crystal and six pale pink rocaille beads.

3 Now thread on one bright pink crystal, two lilac rocaille beads, one clear glass bead, one lilac rocaille bead, one bright pink crystal, one lilac rocaille bead, one pale pink plastic bead, one lilac rocaille bead, one bright pink plastic bead, one purple plastic bead and one bright pink plastic bead.

4 Continue threading on this sequence of beads until you have used all the beads. Remove the stop bead.

5 Refer to the Fixing calottes and Fixing a necklace clasp techniques on pages 27 and 22 respectively to finish the necklace with calottes, jump rings and a torpedo clasp.

▲ Long pink leaf necklace

This long, vibrant necklace is worked in a sequence of six light pink freshwater pearls then four bright pink round discs. The holes in the discs are drilled off-centre so they fit together in a jaunty fashion. Three leaf shape drop beads are interspersed amongst the pearls.

▲ Long double strung necklace

An unusual mauve and green colour combination works well on this bohemian necklace. 1.2-cm (^{1}/2-in) diameter beads are strung between purple bugle beads and 4-mm (^{5}/32-in) diameter green beads. A second string of rocaille and larger beads are then threaded between the 1.2-cm (^{1}/2-in) diameter beads.

◀ Long grey necklace

Long, elegant gunmetal grey beads are threaded between pairs of clear glass beads to make this dramatic necklace.

▲ Long pinned necklace

Glass, plastic and crystal beads in all sorts of shapes and sizes are pinned together to make a 120-cm (47-in) long necklace of warm ochre shades. The necklace has an 8-mm (^{5}/32-in) jump ring at the centre. From the jump ring two pinned beads suspending a flat square bead on a head pin are hung.

Suede strand necklace

Suede strand necklace

Water provides the beautiful natural materials for this unusual necklace.

Shells, mother-of-pearl discs and delicately coloured fresh water pearls

are threaded onto tiger tail. Suede thongs hang from the necklace

on tag ends.

Materials and tools

180 cm (2 yd) 3-mm ($^1/_8$-in) wide flat beige suede thong

All-purpose household glue

Superglue

7 silver tag ends

15 x 2-cm ($^3/_4$-in) diameter mother-of-pearl discs

17 x 6-mm ($^1/_4$-in) silver jump rings

70 cm (27$^1/_2$ in) tiger tail

32 peach coloured fresh water pearls

2 silver crimps

16 x 1.5-cm ($^5/_8$-in) diameter shells with holes drilled side-to-side

Silver toggle necklace clasp

Scissors

Cocktail stick

Snipe-nose pliers

Round-nose pliers

Crimping pliers

Wire cutters

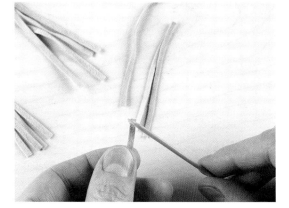

1 Cut twenty-eight 6.5-cm (2$^1/_2$-in) lengths of suede thong. Glue the lengths in seven groups of four, one on top of the other at one end with all-purpose household glue, using a cocktail stick to apply the glue sparingly.

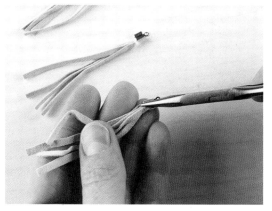

2 Glue the glued ends of the thongs onto a tag end with superglue. Fold over the sides of the tag ends with a pair of snipe-nose pliers, referring to the Fixing a tag end technique on page 27.

3 Slip the hole of each mother-of-pearl disc onto a jump ring. Slip the tag end of the thongs onto the jump rings of seven discs so the thongs hang in front of the discs. Close all the jump rings with two pairs of pliers.

4 Thread a pearl onto the tiger tail. Thread on a sequence of one shell, one pearl, the jump ring of one mother-of-pearl disc without thongs on a tag end and one pearl four times.

5 Thread on a sequence of one shell, one pearl, the jump ring of one mother-of-pearl disc with thongs on a tag end and one pearl seven times.

6 Thread on a sequence of one shell, one pearl, the jump ring of one mother-of-pearl disc without thongs on a tag end and one pearl four times. Thread on one shell and one pearl.

7 Thread a crimp then a jump ring onto one end of the tiger tail. Thread the tiger tail back through the crimp.

8 Adjust the crimp to sit 4 mm ($^5/_{32}$ in) from the jump ring. Secure the crimp with crimping pliers, referring to the Fixing crimps technique on page 21.

9 Push the beads along the tiger tail. Repeat Steps 7 and 8 at the other end of the tiger tail. Open the jump rings and slip each ring onto the ring of the necklace clasp. Close the jump rings with two pairs of pliers.

Beader's tip

Squeeze the glued ends of the thongs with a pair of snipe-nose pliers to make them as flat as possible. This will make them easier to fit neatly into the tag ends.

▼ Mother-of-pearl pendant

A bold rectangular mother-of-pearl pendant hangs on a pendant holder at the centre of this pretty necklace of rose quartz chips. There are a pair of shell staves each side of the centre and iridescent silver beads threaded between the chips. Three 10-cm (4-in) lengths of silver leather thong are tied to each side of the necklace between the staves and iridescent silver beads.

▼ Peacock feather necklace

This dramatic necklace is not for the faint hearted. Nine sets of ten peacock feather strands are fixed to copper tag ends on jump rings and threaded between assorted colourful glass beads. The ends of the necklace are threaded with matt effect green and dark purple beads and fastens with a smart copper ring and bar.

▲ Turquoise thong necklace

Five single turquoise suede thongs are suspended on tag ends between shell staves on this bold necklace. The staves are threaded on tiger tail and interspersed with turquoise glass beads and fixed with crimps and jump rings between silver discs with a hole at each side. The necklace fastens with turquoise thongs fixed on tag ends.

▲ Pink feather necklace

This funky necklace of the brightest feathers would be great to wear for a flamboyant party. Five sets of pink marabou feather and two lengths of pink suede thong are fixed to a tag end. The tag ends hang on jump rings between pink plastic pinned beads which are fixed between silver discs with a hole at each side. Each end of the necklace hangs from suede thong, which is neatened with a tag end at each end and fastens with jump rings and a lobster claw necklace fastening.

Multi-cord necklace

This dramatic necklace has three rows of glass coin beads suspended on coloured cords from pretty filigree end bars. The beads are threaded between small grey beads on wire which will hold the broad shape.

Materials and tools

Gauge 24 silver wire

18 x 3-mm ($^1/8$-in) grey beads

15 x 2-cm ($^3/4$-in) diameter blue/green glass coin beads

110 cm (43$^1/2$ in) pale blue cord

All-purpose household glue

Superglue

12 silver tag ends

14 x 5-mm ($^1/4$-in) silver jump rings

2 three-hole filigree end bars

Silver hook and ring necklace fastening

Round-nose pliers

Wire cutters

Embroidery scissors

Snipe-nose pliers

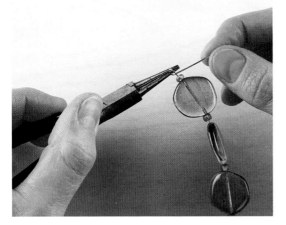

1 Thread a grey bead then a sequence of one coin bead and one grey bead onto wire three times. Make a wrapped loop after the last bead, referring to the Making wrapped loops technique on page 25.

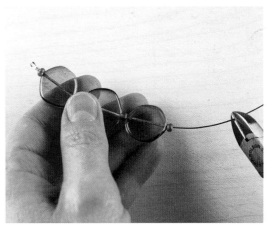

2 Snip the wire 4 cm (1$^1/2$ in) after the last bead and make another wrapped loop.

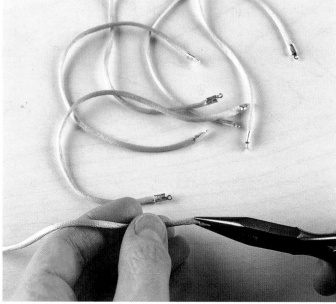

3 For the second row of beads, thread on five coin beads with a grey bead between them and at each end. For the third row, thread on seven coin beads with a grey bead between them and at each end. Make a wrapped loop at each end as before. Bend the wired beads into a gentle curve.

4 Snip six 18-cm (7-in) lengths of cord. Dab all-purpose household glue on the ends to stop them fraying. Glue each end into a tag end with superglue. Fix in place with a pair of snipe-nose pliers, referring to the Fixing a tag end technique on page 27.

5 Fix one end of each tag end to the wrapped loops with a jump ring, opening and closing the ring with two pairs of pliers.

6 Fix the tag ends of the other ends of the cords to the holes of the end bars with jump rings, having the shortest row of beads at the top, the second row in the middle and the third row at the bottom. Fix the necklace fastening to the end bars with jump rings.

▼ Millefiori multi-cord necklace

Three rows of beautiful glass millefiori beads are threaded between small turquoise beads and suspended on turquoise cords from unusual circular end bars.

Beader's tip

The surface of a tag end can become damaged by pliers, wrap a small piece of kitchen towel around the tag end when squeezing it closed to prevent the pliers coming into contact with the metal.

▲ Multi-chain necklace

Here, two rows of fabulous large glass lustre beads are set off by ethnic silver disc beads. The rows of beads hang on chains from two-hole end bars fixed to a necklace fastening.

▶ Mother-of-pearl flower pendant

The three rows of pale beads are threaded on tiger tail so drape in a deeper curve than they would if had they been threaded on wire on this dainty necklace. The top row is made of 4-mm ($^5/_{32}$-in) pearls and silver rocaille beads. The second row is made of frosted plastic beads and the third row is consists of 8-mm ($^5/_{32}$-in) pearls and silver rocaille beads with a lovely mother-of-pearl flower hanging on a triangular pendant holder at the centre. The rows of beads are fixed with crimps and jump rings to three-hole end bars. A single white cord is fixed to each end bar with tag ends and a jump ring and fastens with a hook and ring fastening.

▲ Purple multi-cord necklace

This contemporary necklace has two rows of beads suspended from purple cords. Silver flower shaped spacer beads are pinned between rectangular purple beads. The tag ends at the end of the necklace are fixed to a jump ring each side of the necklace which fastens with a box-and-tongue clasp.

Wired flower necklace

Wired flower necklace

Here is a dramatic floral necklace that uses various techniques. The large
purple flowers are created by wiring slender rice pearls to form the petals.
A variety of other pretty beads are also used to great effect.

Materials and tools

Silver knitting wire

Approx. 26 x 3-mm (^{1}/8-in) diameter
yellow glass beads

Approx. 6 x 6-mm (^{1}/4-in) long lilac
bugle beads

Approx. 3 x 1.5-cm (^{5}/8-in) purple
leaf pendants

Approx. 15 x 5-mm (^{1}/4-in) yellow
miracle beads

Approx. 5 x 1-cm (^{3}/8-in) diameter
white and purple clay flower beads

25 g (1 oz) 3-mm (^{1}/8-in) diameter
white glass beads

18 x 1.2-cm (^{1}/2-in) long purple rice
pearls

18 size 7 white pearl rocaille beads

11 silver crimps

Approx. 5 x 1.2-cm (^{1}/2-in) purple
leaf pendants

3 x 6-mm (^{1}/4-in) silver jump rings

60 cm (24 in) tiger tail

25 g (1 oz) size 11 purple rocaille
beads

Silver barrel necklace clasp

Crimping pliers

Snipe-nose pliers

Round-nose pliers

1 To make the central branch, snip
one 70-cm (27^1/2-in) length of
wire. Thread a yellow glass bead
onto the centre of the wire. Bring
the wires together over the bead
and twist them together for 8 mm
(^{5}/16 in). You now have two wires
which will be referred to as the first
and second wires.

2 Thread a yellow glass bead onto
the first wire. Hold the bead 1 cm
(^{3}/8 in) along the wire. Twist the first
wire on itself over the bead until you
reach the second wire. Now thread
a yellow glass bead onto the second
wire. Hold the bead 1 cm (^{3}/8 in)
along the wire as before. Twist the
wire on itself over the bead until you
reach the first wire. Twist both wires
together for 8 mm (^{5}/16 in).

3 Thread a lilac bugle bead onto the
first wire. Hold the bead 3 mm
(^{1}/8 in) along the wire. Fold the
first wire over the bead and twist
it on itself over the bead until you
reach the second wire. Repeat to
attach two more bugle beads.

4 Twist both wires together for 8 mm (⁵/₁₆ in). Thread a 1.5-cm (⁵/₈-in) leaf pendant onto one wire. Twist both wires together for 5 mm (¹/₄ in).

5 Thread a yellow miracle bead onto the second wire. Hold the bead 1 cm (³/₈ in) along the wire. Twist the second wire on itself over the bead until you reach the first wire. Twist both wires together for 5 mm (¹/₄ in). Repeat to fix a second miracle bead in place.

6 Twist both wires together for 5 mm (¹/₄ in). Thread a flower bead onto one wire. Twist both wires together for 1.5 cm (⁵/₈ in) above the flower.

7 To make the petals of the wired flower, thread a rice pearl then a pearl rocaille bead onto the first wire. Push the beads along the wire to the twisted wires. Insert the wire back through the seed pearl. Pull the wire so the rocaille bead sits on top of the seed pearl. Repeat to fix two more petals on the first wire and three petals on the second wire.

8 Splay open the petals. Twist the wires together on the underside of the wired flower. Bring the longest wire over the front of the flower and thread on a miracle bead. Adjust the bead to sit on the centre of the flower. Take the wire to the underside of the flower and twist both wires together to the end of the wires.

9 Insert the twisted wires through a crimp. Pull the twisted wire back through the crimp, leaving a short loop of wire. Secure the crimp with crimping pliers (see the Fixing crimps technique on page 21).

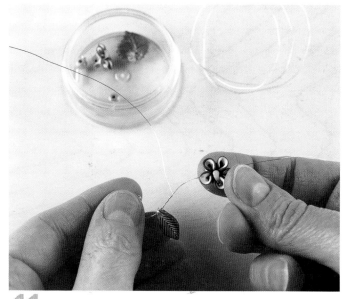

10 Snip two 65-cm (25¹/₂-in) lengths of wire. Use each length to make a 5-cm (2-in) long branch, vary the arrangement of beads and make a wired flower at the top. Finish with a crimp and loop as before.

11 Snip two 40-cm (16-in) lengths of wire. Make two 4-cm (1¹/₂-in) long branches, varying the arrangement of beads used. Finish each branch with a crimp and loop.

12 Snip four 20-cm (8-in) lengths of wire. Refer to Steps 1 and 2 to fix three miracle beads to the centre of two wires. Refer to Step 3 to fix three bugle beads to the centre of the other wires. Twist the extending wires together. Finish with a crimp and loop as before.

13 Thread the central branch onto the centre of the tiger tail. At each side, thread on a sequence of one yellow glass bead and one purple rocaille bead six times. Thread on a yellow glass bead. Thread on the 5-cm (2-in) long branch.

14 Thread on a sequence of one white glass bead and one purple rocaille bead five times. Thread on a white glass bead. Thread on the 4-cm (1½-in) branch. Hang a 1.5-cm (5/8-in) leaf pendant on a jump ring. Continue threading on the hanging miracle beads, hanging bugle beads and leaf pendants amongst alternating purple rocaille beads and white glass beads for 7.5 cm (3 in) each side of the central branch.

15 Thread alternating purple rocaille beads and white glass beads on each side of the necklace for 15 cm (6 in). Thread a crimp then a jump ring onto one end of the tiger tail. Pull the tiger tail back through the crimp. Adjust the crimp to sit after the last bead and the jump ring 3 mm (1/8 in) from the crimp. Secure the crimp with crimping pliers. Snip off the excess wire. Repeat at the other end of the necklace. Fix the necklace clasp to the jump rings.

▲ Wired pink flower necklace

Pretty hanging branches are threaded onto turquoise waxed twine to create this colourful necklace. Single blue beads are threaded through flat pink plastic flower shaped beads on the branches. The large flowers at the top of the branches have two stamens of a pale green bugle bead with blue rocaille bead worked in the same way as the petals of a wired flower. A single flower bead with a blue bead at the centre hangs each side of the branches. The wired pieces hang from the string with a crimp at each side. A few blue beads are threaded onto the string. The ends of the string are finished by threading on a crimp, a blue bead and another crimp. The crimps are secured in place sandwiching the bead.

▲ Green and white wired flower necklace

Make this necklace in pretty spring colours. The large flower is made of white rice pearls with light green rocaille beads at the tips and a large pale green pearl at the centre. A clay triple flower bead hangs on a head pin with pale green and white pearls and light green rocaille beads below the large flower. A shorter head pin with a clay triple flower bead hangs each side of the centre amongst clear and light green rocaille beads and large pale green and white pearls.

▲ Silver and glass wired flower necklace

This antique style necklace has five wired flowers of three petals hanging on a necklace of silver rocaille beads and 3-mm (1/8-in) glass beads. The petals are created with glass teardrop shaped beads.

Beader's tip

If you do not have the required colour beads, paint white beads with coloured nail varnish.

▶ Pearl and wood wired flower necklace

Here, pearls and wood are combined to great effect. The wired flower has five petals of 2.5-cm (1-in) long slender fawn wooden beads with brown pearls. The flower hangs on two 68-cm (27-in) lengths of black tiger tail. At each side of the flower, a pearl and wooden bead is threaded onto one length of tiger tail and 15 fawn rocaille beads on the other. Both tiger tails are then threaded through a black crimp and crimped together. The tiger tails are threaded and crimped together in this way with rocaille beads on one tiger tail and wooden beads and pearls or just pearls on the other. The ends are crimped together enclosing a jump ring. Narrow brown ribbon is sewn to each jump ring.